How *is* Fintech Breaking Barriers *and* Reshaping *the* Future *of* Financial Sevices?

CONNECTING FINTECH

Building Techno-Financial Bridge Using **5D Model**

AF499173

KRISHNA POTNIS

Worldwide Published by
Pendown Press

PENDOWN PRESS LLP
An ISO 9001 & ISO 14001 Certified Co.,
Regd. Office: 3767A, Kanhaiya Nagar,
Tri Nagar, Delhi-110035
Ph.: 8130886000, 9650072927, 8595249536
E-mail: info@pendownpress.com
Branch Office: 1A/2A, 20, Hari Sadan, Ansari Road,
Daryaganj, New Delhi-110002
Ph.: 011-45794768
Website: PendownPress.com

First Edition: 2023
Price: ₹599/-
ISBN: 978-93-5554-706-4

All Rights Reserved
All the ideas and thoughts in this book are given by the author and he is responsible for the treatise, facts and dialogues used in this book. He is also responsible for the used pictures and the permission to use them in this book. Copyright of this book is reserved with the author. The publisher does not have any responsibility for the above-mentioned matters. No part of this publication may be reproduced, distributed, or transmitted in any form or by any means, including photocopying, recording, or other electronic or mechanical methods, without the prior written permission of the publisher and author.
Layout and Cover Designed by Pendown Graphics Team
Printed and Bound in India by Thomson Press India Ltd.

How *is* Fintech Breaking Barriers *and* Reshaping *the* Future *of* Financial Sevices?

CONNECTING FINTECH

Building Techno-Financial Bridge Using **5D Model**

I dedicate this book to my parents
Mrs. Shilpa Suresh Potnis
and Late Mr. Suresh Krishnarao Potnis,
whose love, care, and nurturing have brought
me to the level where I stand today.

Their unwavering support and value system
inculcated in me are my greatest
sources of strength.

Contents

Preface

Are you in the financial technology sector or trying to get into the financial technology sector?

Want to know the evolution of Fintech, Fintech domains and technological development in the Fintech sector?

If you are reading this book, chances are you have an interest in learning more about the Fintech phenomenon, which is taking the world by storm. This book will help you to know the barriers and impediments in the Fintech evolution and explore these in order to be able to address them for reshaping the future of financial services.

The book explores the connection of technology evolving into the financial sector to service consumer needs through the generations and also understands the Fintech Market size and potential. The book shows you how this magical connection between finance and technology is impacting individual lives and society as a whole.

This book is aimed at understanding practical approaches for Fintech evolution, trends and disruptions and new and futuristic technology models.

The simple formulation of the 5D model explains the ongoing and upcoming trends in the Fintech domain like.

Democratisation of Finance

Understanding how the solutions are being built to reuse assets across the supplier and consumer.

- **Decentralisation of Finance:** Can completely turn the global economy on its head by making the finance sector transparent and more easily accessible.
- **Disruptions:** Upcoming trend of disruptions in the Fintech industry.
- **Directive Regulatory:** Regulating the Fintech industry is essential as it navigates speedy growth.
- **Data-Driven:** Understanding Data usage and its impact on Fintech

Finally, the book concludes with the sharing of an inspired thought about Design Thinking being the way forward for the Fintech industry.

Acknowledgement

My deepest appreciation and gratitude go to my loving wife, Varsha, for her support throughout this journey. I am thankful to my sons, Adit and Neil, for their ever-enthusiastic discussions during the book-writing process. They have been a constant source of energy.

I would also like to thank my mentors, especially Mr. Bhuwan Pant, for always encouraging me to think out of the box.

Also, this book would not have been possible without support from Lars Marlow Krosby and Afreen Mulla and the team at Verifone.

Finally, I would like to express my gratitude to my family and the countless experts, colleagues, and friends who have shared their knowledge and experiences with me. Your contributions have been invaluable, and I couldn't have completed this book without you.

This list would be incomplete if I did not thank my publisher Mr. Dinesh Verma, Pendown Press and their entire team for their smooth publishing support.

Thank you all from the bottom of my heart.

Many examples, anecdotes, and stories shared in this book result from a collection spanning nearly four decades. They have been collected from various sources like magazines, newspapers, LinkedIn, Twitter, WhatsApp, other speakers, and business meetings, among others.

Unfortunately, sources were not always available or always noted down. So it is impossible to provide an accurate acknowledgement. Regardless of the source, I wish to express my gratitude to all those who have contributed to the book directly, indirectly or anonymously.

Every effort has been made to give credit where it is due for the material contained herein. If I inadvertently omitted to credit someone, it shall be rectified in future publications if brought to my attention.

Humankind is creature of financial habits.

Chapter 1

The Magical Connection

The majority of us who aren't Gen Z or Gen Next were born and grew up in a world where our parents seldom used financial services.

I remember going to the bank with my father to update the passbook and withdraw money for monthly expenses. This used to be an exciting experience. Especially the first week of the month when there were long queues for withdrawing money and even separate queues for printing the passbook. I am sure many of you can relate to this scenario.

It is a very nostalgic feeling as I am writing this. Those times were completely different. There were insurance agents who visited homes for life but rarely for health insurance.

Utility bills were also a completely different ball game than what they are today. They were paid by visiting specific centres, for example, you had to visit the electricity board office for payments of electric bills, the telephone office for paying telephone bills and all other such utilities.

Stock market investments were a rarity, too and could only be done by filling out a bunch of forms and visiting a broker. All these payments were predominantly in either cheques or cash, which was the normal way of life back then. Pondering further on this makes me realise how disjointed and isolated all these financial aspects were. Also, there were so many non-financial aspects of these transactions.

Today our world is completely different, and all these financial services are well-connected. The silos are breaking away. Finance & Technology have gravitated towards each other.

Brett King, an Australian author, speaker, and futurist in the field of financial technology, known for his expertise and thought leadership in the intersection of banking, technology, and customer experience, has been emphasising that.

"The intersection
of technology
and finance is where
the real magic happens."

I am pretty sure that, like me, you have no two opinions about this statement.

Today we navigate the world of finance & financial services sitting right where we are through a mere click of our fingers & all of the financial services we are using are based on digital technology. Let us dive into this magical new world to understand how exactly Finance and Technology are connected.

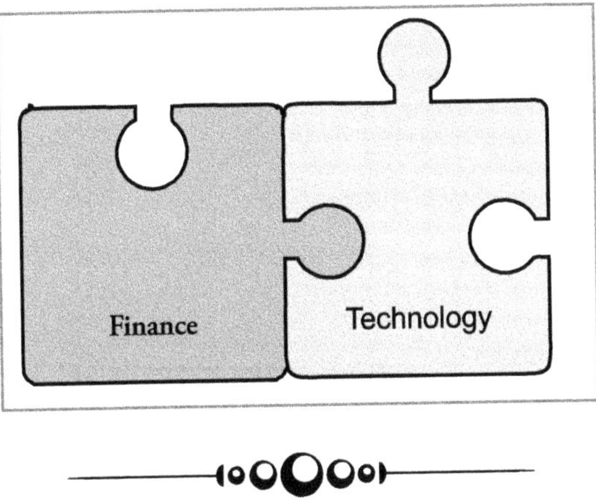

Innovation fuels Fintech's growth.

Chapter 2

Decoding The Fintech Industry

$54 Million

The average funding deal for a Fintech Startup in 2020.

(Source: Venture Scanner)

$105.3 Billion

Global Fintech Investment in 2020. (Source: KPMG)

50,000 Technologists employed by JPMorgan. (Source: Reuters)

The need for Fintech Professionals increased by 42% by the end of 2020. (Source: THE ECONOMIC TIMES)

The Indian Fintech Market is expected to reach INR 6,207 Billion by 2025. (Source: BFSI.com)

India tops Fintech adoption at 87% in 2019. (Source: GARTNER)

Demand for virtual cards shot up by approximately 600% amidst the Covid-19 crisis. (Source: TechCabal)

Amazed by the facts? I am sure you are!

The above facts and figures undoubtedly prove that the Fintech Industry is reaching sky-high!

It is, indeed, the new Gold Rush.

But the Billion Dollar Question here is:

What are you doing to leverage this golden opportunity?

So, dear readers, Fintech has proven to be more than just a buzzword, a fad, or a trend. It is one of the hottest industries in the world today.

Anybody who is remotely connected to the field wants to jump on to the Fintech Bandwagon, so tell me, what are you doing to ensure that you benefit from this emerging technology and stay at the forefront of the Fintech revolution?

Lost for words & not clear about decoding & leveraging this revolutionary opportunity to the fullest???

Well, I've got great news for you; That is where this book comes in—

This book is designed for professional Fintech enthusiasts who are interested in gaining a deeper understanding of Fintech trends, ecosystems, tools, and methods of the latest financial technology innovations.

If you are already a Fintech professional for an extended period of time and have built and delivered Fintech systems across sectors, then congratulations! You are already mining the golden Fintech opportunity to the fullest, and you may put this book down and carry on with whatever you were doing.

However, this book will be of significant value to others who aspire to be successful Fintech professionals like you:

Particularly those in the following roles:

- Mid- to Senior-level managers and Fintech enthusiasts working in banking, investment, real estate, insurance, risk management, regulatory, and other fields in the financial industry.
- CXOs who are getting into the Fintech industry to grow their company by gaining knowledge of Fintech that can add value to their enterprise.
- Consultants seeking to create cutting-edge understanding for their clients in the Fintech space.
- Anyone interested in a 'ticket' for the numerous lucrative opportunities in today's hottest industry, whether for leading a Fintech function, starting a Fintech venture or investing in similar ideas.

2.1. The EARN Model

This book is organised in a unique manner that is easy to understand and will help you decode & leverage the Fintech Industry and ride the prosperity wave of Fintech smoothly and profitably.

This unique manner of organising the book is the EARN Model, and it helps explain the Fintech evolution and development cycles.

The core concept to make a note of here is that this is a cyclic process that repeats again and again as and when there are external disruptions.

EARN stands for:

- Evolution
- Arising trends
- Rapid disruptions
- Now and future models

This can be clearly understood from the cyclic diagram shared below.

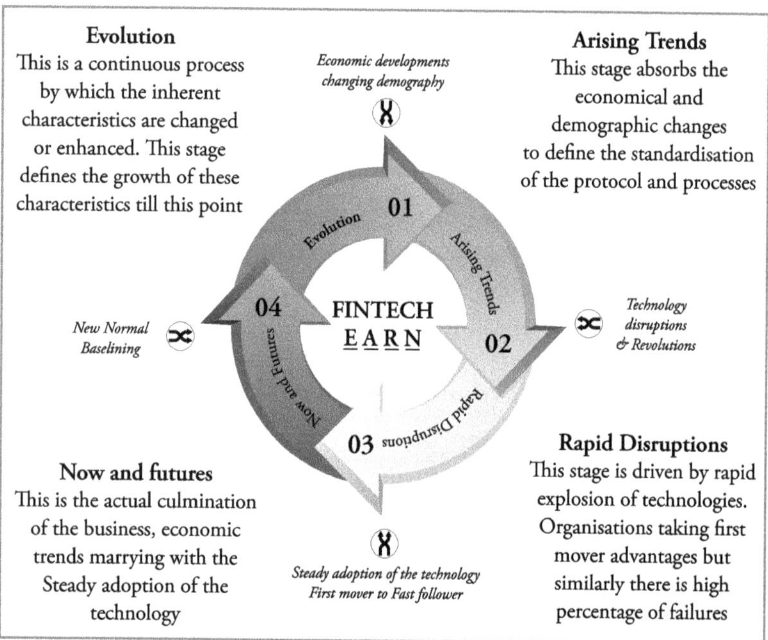

The above diagram is self-explanatory, showing the 4 stages of the EARN Model. Additionally, there are external disruptive forces shown that work as triggers for transitioning into the next stage of the cycle.

The subsequent sections of the book will zoom in on these stages and also the external disruptive forces that change the direction of the cycle to give you a complete understanding of the Fintech Universe.

Evolution tests, refines, and paves the way for a better future.

Chapter 3

Evolution of Fintech

In order to be successful at anything; it s important to understand it thoroughly and to understand it thoroughly, it is important to start from the origin. Therefore in this section, we will take a journey into the genesis and evolution of Fintech.

3.1. Genesis of Fintech

Although in today's day and age, we relate Fintech with the hi-tech industry. This may not be doing true justice to financial technology that existed even before the advent of technology.

Let us understand the meaning of finance - in common understanding, finance denotes managing money, bank, or investments, i.e. anything related to monetary resources and funds.

The etymology of finance

(n.)

c. 1400, "an end, settlement, retribution," from Old French finance "end, ending; pardon, remission; payment, expense; settlement of a debt" (13c.), noun of action from finer "to end, settle a dispute or debt," from fin (see fine (n.)). Compare Medieval Latin finis "a payment in settlement, fine or tax."

The notion is of "ending" (by satisfying) something that is due (compare Greek telos "end;" plural tele "services due, dues exacted by the state, financial means"). The French senses gradually were brought into English: "ransom" (mid-15c.), "taxation" (late 15c.); the sense of "management of money, science of monetary business" first recorded in English 1770.

finance (v.)

late 15c., "to ransom" (obsolete), from finance (n.). Sense of "to manage money" is recorded from 1827; that of "to furnish with money" is from 1866. Related: Financed; financing.

Entries linking to finance

fine (n.)

c. 1200, "termination, end; end of life," from Old French fin "end, limit, boundary; death; fee, payment, finance, money" (10c.), from Latin finis "end" (see finish (v.)), in Mediaeval Latin also "payment in settlement, fine or tax."

Modern meaning "exaction of money payment for an offence or dereliction" is via sense of "sum of money paid for exemption from punishment or to compensate for injury" (mid-14c., from the same sense in Anglo-French, late 13c.) and from phrases such as to make fine "make one's peace, settle a matter" (c. 1300). Me*aning "sum of money imp*osed as penalty for some offence" is first recorded in the 1520s. *Ref: www.etymonline.com*

Let us get into the evolution of the Fintech industry.

3.2 The Fintech Industry: A Historical Overview

The following picture provides a high level of view of the Fintech Generations.

We will explore these topics over the next chapters of the book.

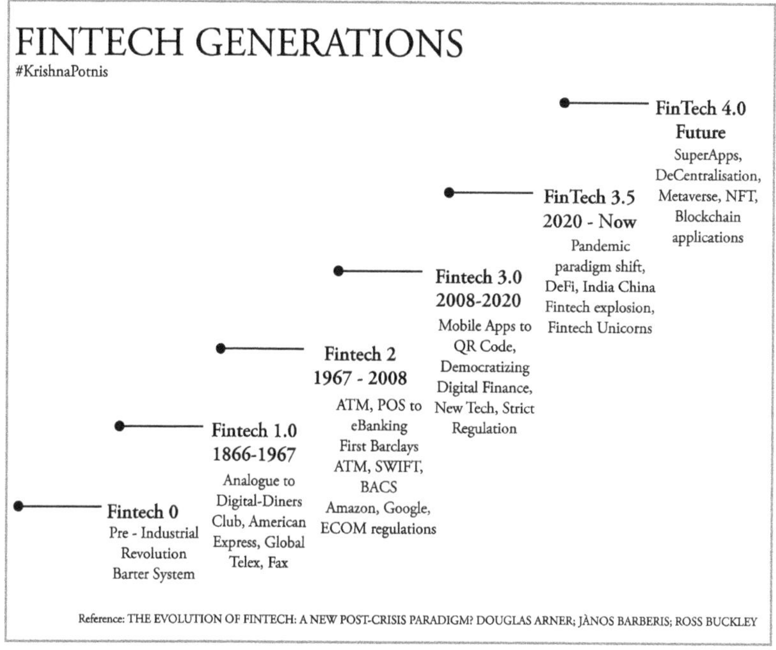

*This closely follows the overall history of Industry 4.0.

3.3 So....What exactly is Fintech?

Good question that!

The world and its cousins are screaming Fintech. It's literally the new gold rush; we've taken a look at its origin & history, but hey, let's pause for a moment and see whether we truly understand what Fintech is.

Before discussing how Fintech is transforming the financial sector and affecting the lives of millions of people, we need to understand what Fintech is.

Managing finances has always been a challenge for businesses and people. Additionally, performing financial transactions has been cumbersome and tedious. With the advent of technology, new approaches are being discovered to address these laborious processes in financial transactions.

Any technology used in the financial industry is referred to as "Fintech".

This includes gadgets from computers to mobile phones.

To put it in simple words,

The term Fintech denotes the usage of technology in the financial sector to make it more responsive, fast, and automotive.

This emerging Fintech Revolution today has had a significant impact on money management and is anticipated to reach an investment value beyond 310 billion through 2022-2023.

Big players like PayPal, Google, Apple, Meta and also different government agencies have been investing heavily in the sector.

According to the BCG data, the number of Fintech startups around the world tripled during the pandemic, and the number stood at about 26,000 in 2021.

Today almost 96% of consumers are aware of Fintech services, with the majority of them actually using these services.

So how was such a feat achieved, and how is it impacting the financial sector?

3.4 How is Fintech Transforming Finance?

Financial Institutions have the challenging task of providing customers with efficient and transparent services while needing to avoid a range of risks and potential threats. It is a tightrope they walk constantly.

To successfully achieve this, they need to keep their services updated and appealing by incorporating the latest and best technologies available with little impact on the cost of providing the service. Businesses need to keep up with growing market demands as Fintech penetrates the financial sector in a wide range of areas.

But how exactly is Fintech impacting financial services? Let's find out—

Since the rise of Fintech, businesses and individuals are being offered multiple avenues for managing their finances. Namely, customers can manage their financial accounts from anywhere in the world and also trade in marketplaces like stock exchanges or crypto exchanges.

Also, due to the Fintech revolution, people are more aware of tax laws and deductions. These avenues also support regional tax regulations and data privacy laws. Enabling customers to appreciate a single view of the financial trade as well as corresponding liabilities related to the trade.

(a) Better Customer Service

Fintech institutions are rolling out feature-rich personalised apps and offering exclusive services to their customers. Artificial Intelligence (AI) chatbots and robo-advisors have been implemented for providing real-time customer service. The turnaround time(TAT)s of customer queries has been drastically reduced, thereby saving time and increasing customer satisfaction.

(b) Omnichannel Presence

Isn't it convenient that customers no longer have to visit their bank in person? Instead, they can easily handle money transfers, deposits and other payments using their electronic device - computer or mobile apps. With this technological advancement, institutions are saving time and money and investing these to enrich their product offerings/services to customers resulting in higher revenue with better customer satisfaction.

(c) Easy Lending

Fintech has also streamlined the process of lending seamless credit risk assessments and accelerating the loan approval processes. Lending applications are now available to billions of people in the world at their fingertips, New data points and risk modelling capabilities are allowing credit access to people who previously couldn't get credit. Consumers can also request their credit report from credit agencies multiple times a year without having their score affected, thus improving the transparency of the entire lending process. This benefits both the customers and financial institutions, essentially improving economic demography.

(d) Insurance

While it still falls under the umbrella of Fintech, "Insurtech" is rapidly becoming its own industry. The insurance industry continues to follow a slow adoption curve as Fintech startups partner with traditional insurers to automate processes and expand coverage.

Customers can easily compare different insurance policies on their mobile phones and pick the right one at their convenience. Additionally, the claim processes are also optimised via applications instead of visiting the insurance company office. Technological advancements make this insurance issuance and claim processing a very impersonal and impartial mechanism.

3.5. The Digital Payments Revolution

One of the key aspects of Fintech innovation is digital payments. We will go through the digital payments revolution in brief in this section.

Digital payment is the cornerstone of the Fintech industry, moving one step ahead. Digital payments are a mandatory ingredient of any modern-day solution. You cannot imagine a solution without it. Be it Edutech or a FoodTech sector, digital payment has to be an integral part of the solution.

3.5.1 Early Days of Payments

Let us explore the revolution of modern payments.

1920

As per the recorded history of non-cash payments, the initiation was done around the late 1920s when some of the major oil and big departmental stores in the US started using rectangular metal plates in a leather pouch. The customer name, city, state and account number would be embossed on this metal plate. This would be imprinted on a piece of paper and sent to a particular bank (namely Flatbush National Bank of Brooklyn) for clearing. This is considered as the first issued Charge-it card.

1940

On similar lines as above, different materials were explored to manage cost and increase reliability. Diners Club started issuing their own cards on this basis.

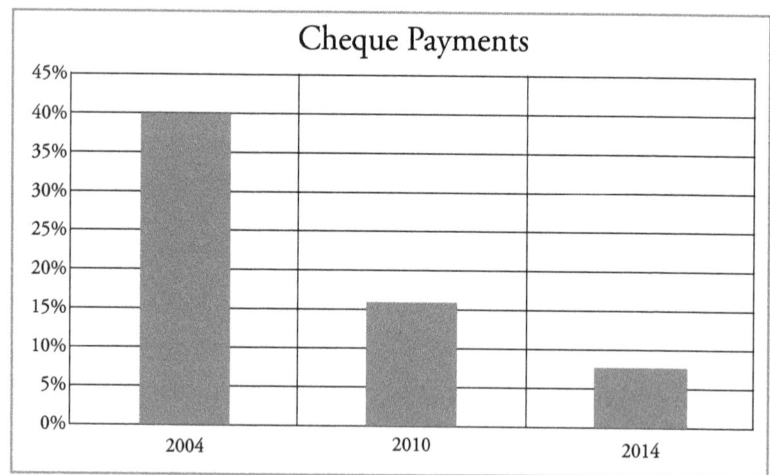

Only a few departmental stores used the embossed card method, as mentioned above. The most prevalent method still was cash and cheque payment in stores.

Some of the recorded events show that the cheque came into existence in the Netherlands during the 1500s. Since the last two decades, cheque payments have declined drastically.

Also, there are countries like the UK and Ireland that tried to modernise the cheque payment option by accepting the photo of the cheque but were not very successful. Now countries like Germany and France don't use cheque payments at all.

3.5.2 Cheque Payment: An Unreliable Mode of Payment.

It is interesting to understand how the revolution happened in the last half-century. Earlier, the only way to pay for goods and services was through cash payments. The logical way ahead was to use the bank account to transfer the money, and the mode adopted for this was using bank cheques that the payer would draw in the name of the payee. Everyone is aware of cheque payments, and this mechanism is still used widely across the world.

The major limitation was that both the payer and payee should have a bank account. During the early 20th century, the overall percentage of banked customers was in single digits. If both the payer and payee had bank accounts, then only the cheque could be tendered.

There were a lot of downsides, and this system was prone to fraud due to the fact that the product or service provider (the payee) was not aware if this cheque was going to get encashed successfully and in time. The payee would need to wait for at least 3-4 days to get any update from the bank, whether the cheque was encashed or not. If there were issues in encashing the cheques, for instance, sufficient balance not available or signature mismatch, then the payee had to contact the payer for another mode of payment.

This was a pretty cumbersome process of selling and buying products and services, especially tracking and reconciling. As a result, the sector pushed for better and more efficient payment methods.

Latest news Published Jun 2023: Australian Banks are phasing out cheques by 2030.

3.5.3 Offline Card Payment: A Baby Step Towards Credit Cards

The next obvious step was to guarantee that the payment was successful. For the product and service provider - the payee must be assured that the payment would definitely be made. It is not only the payer or the buyer who would guarantee payment, but a reputed financial institution must ensure the success of the payment. This was the junction when Credit cards were introduced. These cards were issued by financial institutions to the card holders, i.e. the consumer or the payer.

An old credit card picture with embossed numbers and signature at the back. Actually, the look and feel of these cards have not changed much over the last 40-50 years.

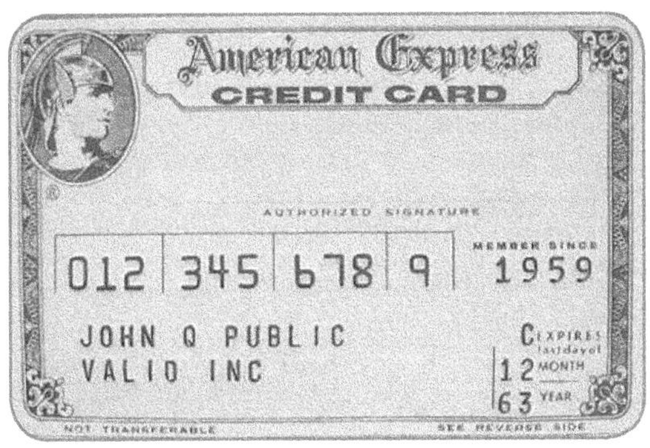

As shown above, these cards had an embossed unique card number with the name of the cardholder, issue number and the cardholder's signature on the strip at the back.

The product and service provider had a business account set up with a financial institution that issued a Card imprint machine to the service provider.

When a consumer visited a business establishment and bought goods and services, this card was presented as the mode of payment. The product/service provider would use a similar machine to take the imprint of the card on a card slip with a carbon copy.

Once the imprint was taken, the customer would sign this slip. The payee would verify the signature with the signature on the backside of the card. At the end of the day, all such slips would be sent by the payee to the financial institution having his account. That, in turn, would process these cards with the consumer banks like any other cheque.

This process addressed concerns such as the need for a third-party guarantor to ensure payment. Additionally, a copy of the slip would also be with the consumer for any dispute management. Essentially this process still has a lot of issues like consumer overspending, lag in the realisation of money and risk of forgery similar to the cheque mechanism.

3.5.4 Additional Verification by Phone

To address overspending and forgery, this process was augmented by a telephone call to the provider to verify whether the card was still valid with the required balance. This improved the buyer and the business owners' overall experience for a smooth execution of the transaction.

3.5.5 The Magnetic Strip - A New Age Invention - First Online Transaction

In 1960, IBM developed a magnetic strip card having unique details of the employees. This was developed for IBM's internal use. Due to the convenience of this mechanism, this was soon popularised and adopted by financial institutions.

In the picture below you will get a complete idea of the specifications of the magnetic strip and the magnetic card reader used by the financial institution.

There would be three distinct tracks on the magnetic stripe: track 1, track 2, and track 3.

Also, there would be additional information on the back of the card as shown below. The front of the card would more or less remain the same as seen in earlier sections.

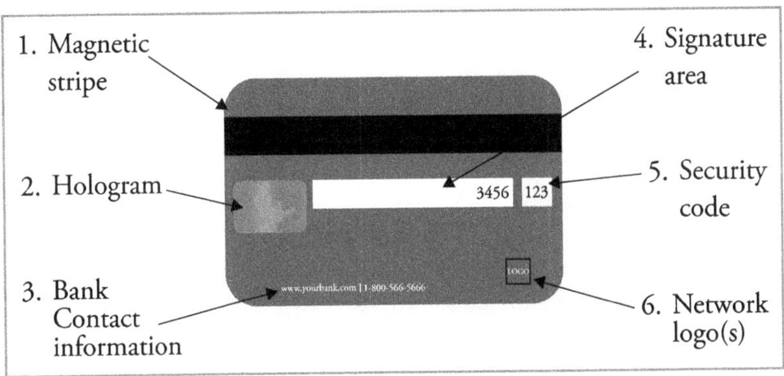

These magnetic cards started circulating in the 1980s for food vending machines, and eventually, ATMs compatible with these magnetic strip cards were developed. Today also we use this mechanism in ATM machines for withdrawing cash or in any other banking transactions with ATM machines.

Summary

Banking and financial services have readily adopted finance technology due to the advent of cutting-edge technologies and easy adaptability. Also, with Fintech, financial institutions can meet customer demands for a safe and convenient banking experience.

As a result of Fintech becoming increasingly popular across all industries, we can expect huge changes within the financial sector. Traditional banks need to utilise these solutions in order to compete effectively and grow their businesses in the future.

The bottom line is that—Globally, the Fintech industry has become a major player in the overall economy, business environment, and fabric of modern society as a whole. A wide category of people are involved in this rapidly growing field, and Fintech is here to stay.

Finance and technology are tracks, with fintech as the racing bullet train.

Chapter 4

Evolution for Fintech Domains and Technology

4.1 Fintech Domains

It is crucial to understand what falls under the umbrella of Fintech. Let us start with a more in-depth understanding of Fintech and identify the Fintech Domains.

Essentially today, Finance is money in motion, i.e. the exchange of worldly goods and services against valuable currency.

We come across the following major financial entities around us, and we interact with these financial institutions every day.

1. **Banks** : These are the pivot point of all finances. Banks offer consumers financial accounts to organise money in a regulated manner.
2. **Insurance** : This has become an integral part of everyone's life lately - From Life insurance, Vehicle insurance to Insurance of valuable goods (e.g. a high-end electronic device) is very prevalent. The essence of insurance is to be covered during any untimely event. This comes at a cost that is paid in full or in parts at the start of the tenure or periodically.

3. **Lending, i.e. loans :** This is one of the largest financial interactions in today's day and age. Everyone occasionally wishes to buy big-ticket items, be it a house, a car or even a fancy electronic gadget. An easy finance loan from a financial institution (Bank or NBFC) is the obvious option. Now this predominantly includes - Home and Car loans, Credit Cards, Short Term Loans, or Buy Now Pay Later Micro Loans. The method of regular repayments, interest on the loan amount and loan tenure are some of the factors governing and influencing this. So we see around us zero per cent EMIs (Equated Monthly Instalments) to high-risk, high-interest loans for buying a car. An interesting fact: "Today in many countries car loan interest rates are similar to education loans" indicates how society's needs are changing.
4. **Wealth :** As we mentioned earlier, the main purpose of banks is to organise money using different instruments such as bank deposits which offer higher interest rates on our money and help its growth. Now because of the market situation, the rate of growth of this deposited money can barely beat inflation. Other instruments evolved to improve bank rates and compete with inflation, and provide better returns on your money. This includes but is not limited to - Stocks, Mutual Funds, FMPs (Fixed Maturity Plans), Bonds and so on. Essentially a person has multiple avenues to invest money so that money can grow with the "Power of Compounding".

5. **Payments :** Today, we use various different mechanisms for paying for goods and services. This predominantly includes - QR Code Payments (BHIM, UP in IndiaI), Credit and Debit Card, Net Banking, Wallet Payments and even Crypto Payments in some countries. These mechanisms are used in offline -brick-and-mortar shops as well as Online portals for online shopping. Easing the way of paying for goods and services, i.e. it is helping to bring the producer and consumer closer than ever before.
6. **Tax :** One of the fundamental parts of every economy is tax. Taxes include - Income Tax, Road Tax, Property Tax, GST, VAT, Toll Tax and so on and so forth. This is the amount defined by government institutions to serve the community at large to provide the facilities and infrastructure for society.

So at a broad level, we can consider the following as the domain Areas of Fintech

The following picture indicates the major Fintech Domains. At this juncture, let us review these at a macro level and in the later sections of the book; we will go into the details of each domain.

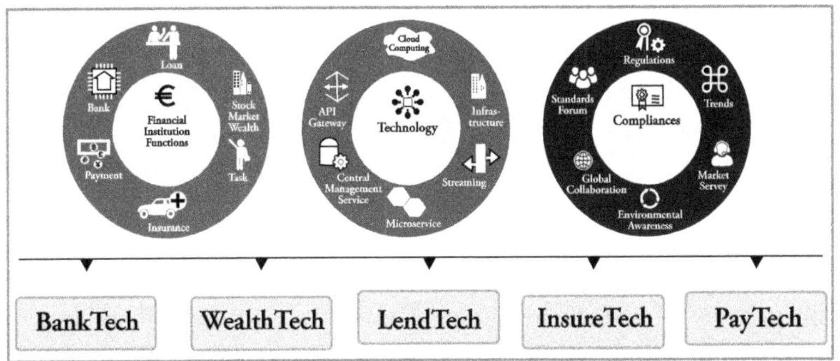

Summary

- The financial sector is an area that has witnessed a major transformation with technological advancements, benefitting both people and businesses. Handling finances had never been an easy task; however, now, with the application of technology to finance, the process has become so convenient.

This is what Fintech is all about—

Combining Finance + Technology to create a Win-Win!

- Financial Institutions and banks are using Fintech to impart a range of facilities - from online banking, loan management, tax calculations & e-filing and insurance buying & management to improve customer services.
- This ease of remote operations is the reason for its success, demand and growth globally! Fintech is touching lives and making finance simpler for the world.

4.2 Applying Technology to Fintech: Tracing the Journey

Moving on, let us quickly look at the second part of Fintech - the "Tech".

As we are all aware, this is the age of technology and information.

Technology, in simple words, is the tools and techniques to ease human life.

In short, we can consider the invention of the "Wheel" as the genesis of the technology. The wheel is where it all began, the desire of humankind to make life easier for themselves through innovation, adaptation & application.

Over hundreds of years, what began as one simple invention, this technology evolved with the advent of Farming and the Industrial Revolution across the world.

While on one hand, the genesis of technology was to make life easier, better and more prosperous, there is another aspect to technology- the use of technology as weapons!

- **Communication Connects the World**

One of the biggest drives to develop technology is the weapons race which has led to two world wars in the last 120 years. While the weapons race in itself is to be condemned, this race has resulted in the development of multiple tools, which culminated in new-age technology. One of the major evolutions is communication - from the Morse code and telephone communication to modern-day internet and satellite connections.

In the last 50 years, there has been a "Silicon Revolution" in which technologies have built feature-rich silicone electronic components. These electronic components enabled us to build calculators, computers and, in recent times, mobile phones.

With the advent of Computers, Mobiles and Communication- humanity stepped further into the age of the "Internet", where all electronic devices could be connected across large distances and communicate on demand.

About forty years ago, a computer programmer was considered at par with a rocket scientist or a brain surgeon. In recent times due to major evolution in software and hardware, programming has become a regular average job. Everyone has the latest computer and mobile at their disposal.

Due to the limitations of time & space, for a focused discussion, we will mention only three predominant aspects of software technologies here.

1. **API:** Application Programming Interface enables two mobiles/computer systems to talk to each other in a common language and exchange valuable information.
2. **Data Store:** This is the repository of all the information exchanged as well as the information of the parties between whom the exchange took place.
3. **Application:** This is a predefined program which manipulates and transforms the data into meaningful information that can be digested by the user.

4.3 TechFin: What Does That Even Mean?

So we've been talking about and understanding the marriage of finance & technology that created the magical world of fintech up until now.

What if we reversed the order of the union and merged technology & finance to create TechFin? What would that mean?

Are Fintech and TechFin one and the same?

Well, a good analogy would be a coin here, a coin has two clear and distinct faces, but they are both joined together to make one identity.

Similarly, FinTech & TechFin can be compared to two faces of the coin that are not the same but work toward facilitating a common purpose.

Before we move further, let's define TechFin—

A technology company that develops hardware and software solutions for the implementation and automation of the business processes connected to the financial industry is referred to as TechFin.

It implies the use of new-age technological advancements and the latest electronic gadgets to push classical methods and devices out of the financial domain. TechFin companies adopt cutting-edge technologies and innovative ways of thinking to provide financial institutions and consumers with the best-in-class services.

Additionally, TechFins also invest in the startup ecosystem to engage in the wider innovation space.

So while FinTech is the macro concept, one can safely say that TechFin is the facilitator of executing and applying that concept.

FinTech is the larger universe, and TechFin is a subset of the same.

Let us flush out the commonalities and stark differences between Fintech companies and TechFin Companies.

Fintech organisations are generally the financial institutions that employ technology (by partnering and hiring technology companies and experts) in bettering their financial services and delivery models. Moreover, these financial institutions are bound by strict regulations and compliances. Hence the technology applications need to follow restrictive frameworks and guidelines.

TechFins, conversely, drive innovation to address peripheral problems in the financial market as well as find newer ways to automate existing financial practices using the latest technological trends. Because of the technology innovations and automation TechFins are always pushing the envelope of regulation. Also, they are ready to find advanced technology mitigations to address compliances that differentiate them from core Fintech organisations.

Let us take a look at the major TechFins changing the world drastically.

4.3.1 Major TechFins Changing the World of Finance

These BigTech firms are equipped with the power and reach necessary to handle these financial issues. Essentially these are regional start-ups that also fall under the TechFin umbrella as they are addressing financial process automation using technology and have blown up and gone global. We will explore the details in the upcoming chapters of the book. For now, let's do an overview.

MAANG- [The US] Meta, Amazon, Apple, Netflix and Google

BAT - [China] Baidu, Alibaba (Ant-Alipay), Tencent (WeChat)

Although Fintech and TechFin can have a different DNA, the majority of the time they work in a Coopetition.

Does Coopetition sound new to you? Well, it's a marker of the way the world of business in general and financial services in particular functions today. Here's more clarity on it.

Coopetition

Coopetition or co-opetition is a neologism coined to describe cooperative competition. Coopetition is a portmanteau of cooperation and competition. Basic principles of co-opetitive structures have been described in game theory, a scientific field that received more attention with the book Theory of Games and Economic Behavior in 1944 and the works of John Forbes Nash on non-cooperative games. Coopetition occurs both at inter-organizational and intra-organizational levels.

–Wikipedia

Fintech and TechFin Organisations work together to provide the best of the services to the market place, e.g. GooglePay - which is a fund transfer and payment innovation from Google which uses the financial institution ecosystem like acquiring banks as the backend to actually make the fund transfers.

4.4 Exploring Fintech - The Fintech Mandala

Ha, I am sure you are wondering what Krishna is up to. Isn't a Mandala a spiritual world? So, why is he bringing it up in a book on Fintech?

I hear you, my friends, be patient, all will be clear to you as we progress.

A mandala is a spiritual and ritual symbol that can be understood in two different ways:

1. Externally as a visual representation of the universe
2. Or internally as a guide for several traditional practices that take place in traditions.

The Mandala belief is that by entering the mandala and proceeding towards its centre, you are guided through the cosmic process of transforming the universe from one of suffering into one of joy and happiness.

This can be applied to successfully navigating the Fintech Cosmos as well.

Mandala

A mandala is a geometric configuration of symbols. In various spiritual traditions, mandalas may be employed to focus the attention of practitioners and adepts, as a spiritual guidance tool, for establishing a sacred space and as an aid to meditation and trance induction. *–Wikipedia*

Apart from Indology wisdom, this concept is also accepted and corroborated by Western Scientists.

"The Universe can not be read until we have learnt the language and become familiar with the characters in which it is written. It is written in Mathematical language, and the letters are triangles, circles and other Geometrical figures, without which means it is humanly impossible to comprehend a single word."

~Galileo Galilei

"We live in a mathematical world or Matrix. The universe is a mathematical correlation between sound and form. All matter is nothing but a mathematical symmetry of vibrations and frequency of energy particles."

- Dr Michio Kaku,
Author of Physics of the Future

Dear readers, the figure below is a clear depiction of the Fintech Mandala that will make it easy for you to understand & navigate the Fintech universe joyfully and successfully.

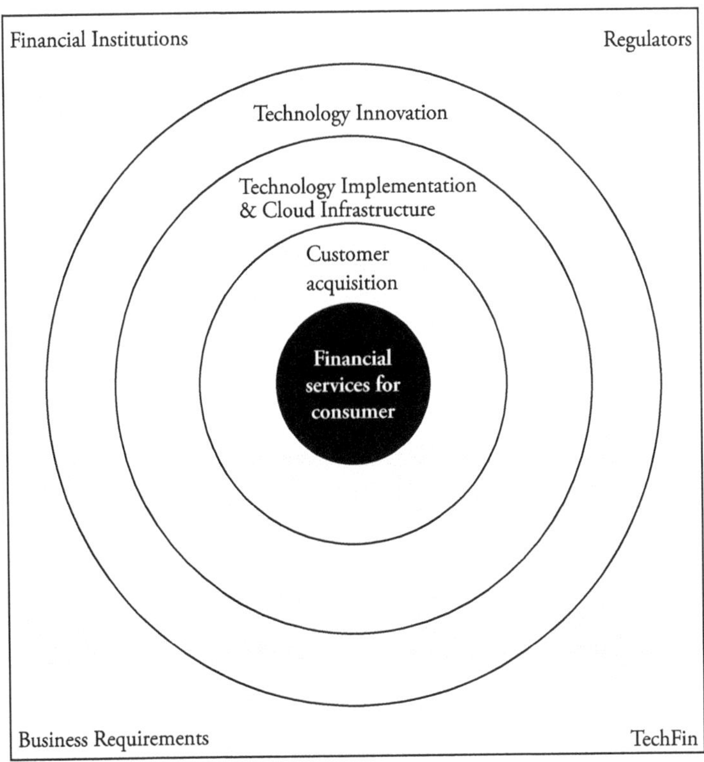

The Fintech mandala above shows

1. The Four Pillars of Fintech - **denoted by the four cardinal corners:**

    a. **Financial institutions:** These are the central banks and the big government/non-government banks responsible for financial movements across multiple entities.

    b. **The Regulators:** These are the institutions - watch dogs per se responsible for overseeing the financial movements, monitoring the senders and receivers for making sure all the compliance requirements, along with security measures, are strictly followed.

    c. **TechFin:** This is a broad term and constitutes technology companies getting into the financial sub-processes. We will be seeing these in detail in later sections.

    d. **Business Requirements:** The sole existence of Financial institutions, regulators and TechFin companies is to facilitate financial services. This is the most dynamic corner of the mandala. As new businesses and ventures are being formed, different financial needs are being raised. This initiates the net components of Mandala to achieve the end consumer service.

2. **Fintech Service Concentric circles:**

    a. **Technology Innovation Circle:** This is the quintessential component of Fintech. Fintech could not exist without this as we have seen in the history of Fintech. This enables tools and techniques development to achieve Fintech services for consumers.

b. **Technology Implementation and Cloud Infrastructure:** This circle indicates the platform and container to execute technology. Including big tech, which is the core area of technology companies. Later in the sections, we will get into the details of these.

c. **Customer Acquisition:** The business requirement corner defines the business use cases indicating the means and modes of financial services exchange. Saying that once the technology implementation is done, the corresponding customer base has to be contacted. Although this process can be initiated much earlier in the life cycle, the actual customer connection cannot happen unless the service implementation is in place and can be consumed.

d. **Financial Service for Consumer:** This is the central consecrated area that serves as a receptacle for the Fintech universe and as a collection point of forces discussed.

4.5. And with Ease, the Problems Manifested

As there are always two sides to a coin, so it is with everything. The ease of doing transactions with the advent of the magnetic strip was followed by a myriad of problems. Here we will look at them in some detail.

4.5.1. Security

With Fintech advancements till the late 1990s, along with the success of the Magnetic Stripe Payments, came the dark side.

The frauds

- This technology and Magnetic strip writers and readers were easily available.
- Fraudsters used these devices to copy the magnetic strips and shop using these forged skimmed cards.
- The number of fraudulent transactions increased exponentially year on year.
- At the height of these financial frauds, there was a fraud every 7 seconds in the US during the year 2000.
- This resulted in a loss of revenue for the banks as the liability of securing these electronic payments was with the banks who issued these magnetic cards and verified these online.
- This prompted a serious need to incorporate stringent security measures.

4.5.2 Centralised Controls

It is important to note that Fintech's ecosystem is controlled by specific financial institutions. This strictly controlled ecosystem presents automatic restrictions on innovations and disruptions.

A rigid, centralised ecosystem does not only present restrictions but also limited communication, stifled creativity, the danger of losing key decision-makers, and inflexible decision-making.

Historically, centralization was desirable in finance as a maintainer and measure of global financial processes stability. It is also thought to be more stable and secure than personal management.

However, the centralised finance sector is not as stable as many think; it is affected by issues such as

- Questionable lending processes
- Forgery,
- Fraud, etc.

Financial institutions that control Fintech need to find the right balance between managing risks and promoting innovations.

While the world economy recovers from the recession due to the pandemic, the stakes can possibly be higher.

- The pace of innovations has picked up, including some ground breaking ones. In the early 2000s, innovations took the form of new products that helped consumers get credit easily, and investors manage risks better and generate higher returns.
- Fintech puts banking and other financial services in the hands of consumers, where they can now make payments, trade stocks, and perform basic banking with apps using mobile phones.
- However, organisations and companies that use disparate systems or outdated business management apps cannot keep up with the world that increasingly focuses on digital technologies.

- The majority of the world owns a gadget, like a smartphone, and can access the internet. But many countries still cannot provide reliable financial accountability or stability and banking accessibility.

4.5.3 Lack of Financial Inclusion

To begin with, Fintech had not permeated almost every walk of life like it has today.

Historically, the Fintech ecosystem included a very small segment of society. To get involved in the ecosystem, specific criteria, including fixed income and financial stability level, were required.

While new financial technologies introduce significant changes in people's lives, most changes compound over time.

Lower financial services fees, higher investment returns, lower borrowing costs, and more savings capacity are critical marginal improvements in the products available to lower-income individuals.

Even today, financial inclusion in developing countries is constrained by the limited ability of financial institutions to overcome risk and cost constraints. The population's lower-income segments are usually considered unbankable due to a lack of formal documentation and small and infrequent transactions.

Two factors hinder Fintech from effectively driving financial inclusion,

1. Lack of partnership with organisations and companies that address the root causes of financial exclusion and

2. Lack of understanding that the factors that drive financial exclusion are usually not themselves. That means there are systemic underlying framework issues that exclude economically challenged populations.

Job opportunities, education level, health, and family circumstances are stronger stability determinants than paychecks that arrive two days earlier or savings Annual Percentage Yield.

Financial technology undoubtedly helps improve and automate services and processes within organisations. On the other hand, different issues with Fintech elevate people's imaginations in new ways while encouraging unparalleled growth.

Nevertheless, just like other things, there is room for improvement.

Summary

- With technological advancements, an area that has witnessed a major transformation is the financial sector, benefitting both people and businesses.
- Handling finances had never been an easy task; however, now, with the application of technology to finance, the process has become so convenient. This is what Fintech is. The use of technology in the financial sector is Fintech.
- Financial institutions and banks are using Fintech to impart a range of facilities - from online banking, managing loans, taxes, and insurance to improved customer services. This is the reason for its success,

demand, and growth globally! Fintech is touching lives and making it simpler for the world.

- This book organised in the Earn Model (Evolution Arising trends Rapid disruptions Now) is meant not just for Fintech enthusiasts but also mid to senior-level professionals in the financial sector, CXOs aspiring to grow their organisation, and Consultants in this field.
- Looking at the figures, Fintech is a fast-growing industry, with investments in Fintech startups reaching $105.3 billion in 2020 worldwide.
- As Fintech is creating new opportunities for consumers and businesses, traditional financial services providers are becoming obsolete. Continuous learning and adapting are what Fintech professionals require to stay ahead of the curve.
- Touching upon the history – substantial progress in technology in the past was propelled by factors such as the farming revolution, the industrial revolution, and the weapons race.
- A major progress in technology has been communication, from the Morse code to the internet and satellite connections.
- The silicon revolution led to the invention of feature-rich electronic components, enabling us to build calculators, computers, and mobile phones.

- Subsequently, with the advent of the internet, these electronic devices have the ability to connect across large distances and communicate when required. Software technologies such as API, data storage, and applications are essential for Fintech applications.

The success of Fintech solutions is closely tied to the success of digital payments.

Chapter 5

Arising Trends - COIN

In this section, we will explore the second component of the EARN Model— Arising Trends.

The term "Arising Trends" means changes that are gaining traction and becoming increasingly significant in Fintech. These trends represent a transformation in the directions, ideas, technologies, and/or behaviours shaping the present and are expected to have a powerful impact on the future.

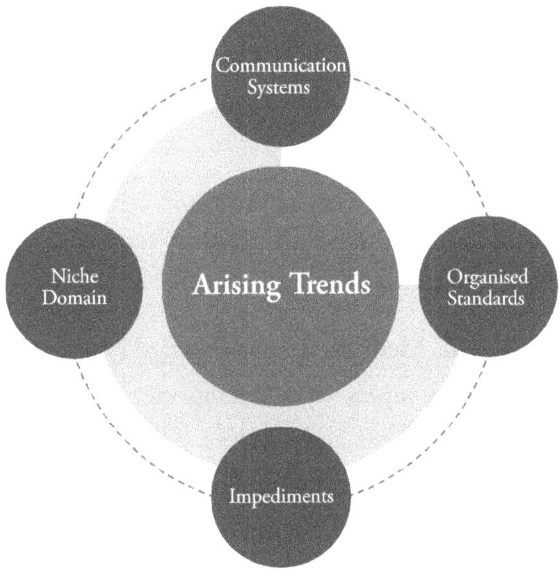

Understanding arising trends in the context of Fintech is crucial for businesses, organisations, and consumers as it allows them to stay connected and adapt to the changing landscape of Fintech. Let us analyse these trends using the Connected systems, Organised standards, Impediments and Niche domains.

5.1. Connected systems

With the dawn of the Internet and the subsequent rapid technological transformation, the standardisation of communication further strengthened its focus on security to ensure maximum certainty and reliability for digital payment consumers.

5.1.1 Fintech ecosystem

The Fintech ecosystem is a connected network of companies, organisations, technologies, and individuals that contribute to the development, growth, and operation of the financial technology industry. It encompasses a wide range of participants, as shown in the diagram below.

- **The Consumer:** This is the most critical component of the ecosystem - the end users of the financial products and services.
- **Small and Medium Companies:** These are innovative startup companies that leverage technology to provide financial products and services. They may focus on areas such as mobile payments, peer-to-peer lending, robo-advisory, blockchain, digital banking, insurtech and more.

- **Large Corporations:** The subsequent sections would provide details about this mover and shaker of the ecosystem. These are the BigTechs who have deep pockets and technology backing to drive the direction of the Fintech industry.
- **Financial Institutions:** Traditional banks and financial institutions play a role in the Fintech ecosystem by either partnering with or acquiring Fintech startups or by developing their own in-house Fintech capabilities. They may collaborate with Fintech firms to enhance customer experience, improve operational efficiency, or offer new digital services.
- **Technology Providers:** Fintech companies rely on various technology providers for infrastructure, software, and tools. This includes cloud computing providers, data analytics platforms, cybersecurity solutions, and other technology enablers.
- **Regulators:** Regulatory bodies and government agencies play a crucial role in shaping the Fintech industry. They establish guidelines, frameworks, and policies to ensure consumer protection and financial stability and promote innovation while maintaining compliance with applicable laws and regulations.
- **Investors:** Venture capital firms, private equity funds, and angel investors provide funding and investment support to Fintech startups and companies. They play a key role in fueling the growth and expansion of the Fintech ecosystem.

- **Innovations via Industry Associations and Communities:** These organisations bring together stakeholders from the Fintech ecosystem to facilitate collaboration, knowledge sharing, and advocacy. They provide a platform for networking, education, and promoting the interests of the Fintech industry as a whole.
- **Government Agencies, Academic and Research Institutions:** Universities, research organisations, and government think tanks contribute to the Fintech ecosystem through research, education, and training programs. They help develop talent, conduct studies, and provide insights on emerging trends and opportunities in Fintech.
- **Global Compliance:** We will see about the regulatory requirements in the subsequent sections; these are the watchdogs of the Fintech ecosystem safeguarding Fintech systems from vulnerabilities

The Fintech ecosystem is dynamic and constantly evolving, driven by technological advancements, changing consumer behaviour, and regulatory developments. It fosters innovation, disruption, and collaboration among various participants to reshape the way financial services are delivered, accessed, and experienced.

Consumer	Access Channel	Capital Conduit	Technology	Disruptors	Regulators
Customers	Small and Medium Businesses	Financial Institutions	Technology Providers (BigTech)	Investors	Government Agencies
Small and Medium Businesses	Large Corporations	Banks	Service Providers	Innovators	Global Compliance

5.2. Organised Standards - Digital Payments

From the time we wake up to the time we arrive at the workplace till the end of the day, we are using a variety of standards, including those for weight, distance and size measurements, to name a few. This is a wonderful thing and a major reason why standards exist, making everyone's life easier every day.

To begin with, let's understand what standards mean—

Standards are published documents that establish technical specifications and procedures intended to increase communication reliability, product behaviour, and methods of operation.

Also, since this book stands on the financial ground, let's understand what a payment standard is specifically—

A payment standard is an agreed-upon norm prescribed by industry, and governments, used by the relevant financial institutions, that outlines the best way to complete a payment transaction end to end.

Payment standards provide a framework that enables various payment points of interactions from diverse vendors to communicate with various financial institutions in a uniform manner.

That's why, for example, a bank payment transaction done in India follows a similar flow as that occurring anywhere in the world. It all happens automatically, behind the scenes, ensuring that our payments are seamlessly processed irrespective of which device, bank and, most importantly, merchant we are interacting with.

Standards provide a stable but continually evolving foundation that enables the entire Fintech industry to develop and thrive.

Think of standards as recipes. By following them, Fintech institutions and Techfins get common interoperability with one another, financial data flows between them, and security of financial information, to name a few.

Financial Standards form the fundamental building blocks for the Fintech industry so that consistent protocols can be established, universally understood and adopted. This helps financial transaction compatibility; interoperability simplifies solution development and speeds time-to-market. Standards also make it easier to understand and compare competing products. As standards are globally adopted and applied in numerous markets, they also fuel international trade.

Meanwhile, when end consumers and businesses are confident that financial transactions will work as expected, they're far more likely to adopt them. Standards-based interoperability also gives them the freedom to mix and match different financial products together to offer a holistic approach for a certain market.

5.2.1 ISO 20022

ISO 20022 is a multi-part International Standard prepared by the ISO Technical Committee TC68 Financial Services. It describes a common platform for the development of messages.

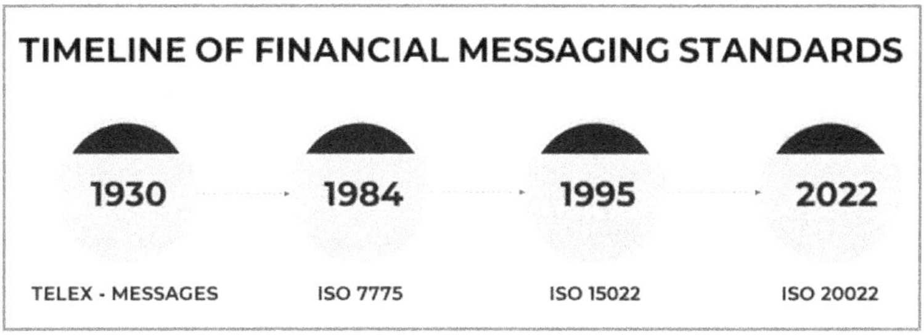

TIMELINE OF FINANCIAL MESSAGING STANDARDS

1930	1984	1995	2022
TELEX - MESSAGES	ISO 7775	ISO 15022	ISO 20022

ISO 20022 is an ISO standard for electronic data interchange between financial institutions. It describes a metadata repository containing descriptions of messages and business processes and a maintenance process for the repository content. The standard covers financial information transferred between financial institutions that includes payment transactions, securities trading and settlement information, credit and debit card transactions and other financial information.

The repository contains a huge amount of financial services metadata that has been shared and standardised across the industry. The metadata is stored in UML (Uniform Modeling Language) models with a special ISO 20022 UML Profile. Underlying all of this is the ISO 20022 metamodel - a model of the models. The UML profile is the metamodel transformed into UML. The metadata is transformed into the syntax of messages used in financial networks. The first syntax supported for messages was XML Schema.

ISO 20022 is widely used in financial services.

ISO 20022 is the successor to ISO 15022; originally, ISO 20022 was called ISO 15022 2nd Edition. ISO 15022 was the successor of ISO 7775.

- **Parts of the standard**

  ISO 20022 Financial services – Universal financial industry message scheme.

  ISO 20022-1:2013 Part 1 Metamodel

  ISO 20022-2:2013 Part 2 UML profile

  ISO 20022-2:2013 Part 3 Modelling

  ISO 20022-2:2013 Part 4 XML Schema generation

  ISO 20022-2:2013 Part 5 Reverse engineering

  ISO 20022-2:2013 Part 6 Message transport characteristics

  ISO 20022-2:2013 Part 7 Registration

  ISO 20022-2:2013 Part 8 ASN.1 generation

5.2.2 ISO 8583

- **The ISO 8583 specification has three parts:**

  Part 1: Messages, data elements, and code values [1]

  Part 2: Application and registration procedures for Institution Identification Codes (IIC) [2]

  Part 3: Maintenance procedures for the aforementioned messages, data elements and code values [3]

A card-based transaction typically travels from a transaction-acquiring device, such as a point-of-sale terminal or an automated teller machine (ATM), through a series of networks, to a card issuing system for authorization against the card holder's account. The transaction data contains information derived from the card (e.g., the card number or cardholder details), the terminal (e.g., the terminal number, the merchant number), the transaction (e.g., the amount), together with other data which may be generated dynamically or added by intervening systems. Based on this information, the card issuing system will either authorise or decline the transaction and generate a response message which must be delivered back to the terminal within a predefined time period.

5.2.3 NEXO

Providing the Building Blocks for Standardisation in Payments Acceptance.

Nexo promotes the widespread acceptance of protocols, a series of standards to ensure interoperability among payment acceptance and acquiring solutions, retail payment solutions, and terminal management systems.

- **The Benefits of the ISO International Standard**

  The ISO International Standard ensures the quality and reliability of goods and services. For businesses, they are strategic tools and guidelines to help companies tackle some of the most demanding challenges of modern business. They ensure that business operations are as efficient as possible, increase productivity and help companies access new markets. For the government, ISO standards draw on international expertise and experience and are, therefore, a vital resource when developing public policy.

- **Shedding Light on the NEXO Standards Protocol**

  Basically, a protocol is a set of rules and specifications to enable two or more entities to exchange information.

The Nexo standards series of protocols belong to the category of application protocols that govern the interaction and exchange of data between software applications. Where the exchange of data is performed between two different pieces of equipment.

The payment terminal (or payment server) located usually at the merchant's location, is a server under the supervision of a bank, payment service provider, or an entity acting on their behalf. It also relies on the use of lower-level data transport protocols to ensure that the exchange of information is carried out in a smooth, secure way.

In the domain of card payments, a protocol enables, among other things, the exchange of information to:

- Authorise a card payment transaction
- Cancel a card payment transaction
- Allow a retailer to be credited for the payment transaction
- Initiate the debiting of the customer (cardholder) account by the bank

NEXO Standards Protocols and the relationships they address.

The NEXO standards portfolio of protocols has been designed specifically to address the lack of open and common specifications today in the market.

5.2.4 QR Code Payments

Consider the year 2010; can you envision a time when you could access funds without even having a credit card or chequebook?

Digitalization has deeply integrated itself into our lives; people have now adapted to the habit of paying or simply buying various items through digital money, either by adding accounts or scanning the QR codes.

Getting into the crux of this, QR codes are also known by the name of quick response code which proficiently reacts to the code that needs to be scanned. It usually consists of squares which are constituted in a square grid in front of a white background. Nowadays, many mobile phones are inbuilt with the feature of scanning, which makes them quite flexible. In other words, QR codes are simple barcodes that store enormous and complex data.

- **The Origin of QR**

  QR codes were basically created for tracking vehicles moving across the assembly line. It was brought into existence in 1994 by Masahiro Hara, Chief Engineer of Denso Wave, a Japanese company manufacturing automatic data capture devices for barcodes.

It is evident that QR codes were generated a long time ago. However, its substantial growth was seen only after the emergence of smartphones. But if we pay keen attention, we would be able to see that even after the smartphones, QR codes couldn't see wide acceptance.

QR codes found a space for themselves and 2017 became the year of a major breakthrough when a top-tier company like Apple decided to integrate a QR reader into its phones after which various manufacturers followed.

Although QR codes were brought into the public domain, users were still not able to adapt to them in a wholesome manner.

However, the year 2020 brought an era where social distancing had to be followed, and people were made to get accustomed to the habit of not being in touch with anything. QR codes in these times acquired a different level of prominence, and people decided to actively use them in every sector such as retail, hospitals, manufacturing, etc.

Now, as we commence further, we need to bring our attention to the two crucial types of QR codes that are usually found and have been in existence-

- **Static QR codes**

  This type of QR code usually doesn't have the ability to be modified. This simply means any error in the added information will require you to repeat the process in order to create a brand new one, However, the thing we should keep in mind is the simple fact that static codes don't expire.

  Such types of static QR codes can be utilised to store identity information.

- **Dynamic QR codes**

  Now, such types of QR codes have the ability to be changed anytime. This happens because the information isn't deeply included in the code itself. It redirects users to a specific URL that can be changed anytime.

  For a brief example, a cafe redirects you to the menu available on their sites.

  One of the most integral benefits of dynamic QR codes is the ability to gather scanning metrics. However, the simple thing that needs to be addressed here is the fact that you can't access personal information from the users; you can see the time, location, and device used for each scan.

  Now, let's keenly decipher how QR codes actually work.

QR codes work in alignment with barcodes found in the supermarket. Each QR code consists of black squares and dots that comprise different information. When a user chooses to scan, the unique code on the barcode translates or simply designs itself into the form of human-readable data.

Furthermore, let's take this opportunity and throw some light onto a few advantages QR codes render-

1. It has the capability of storing large amounts of data.
2. It can be scanned from a screen or paper.
3. It's a safe option as the information can be encrypted.
4. It provides readability even when part of the code is damaged or vague.
5. The spot payments eventually save a decent amount of time.
6. Saves the additional cost as now merchants don't have to invest in any other third-party hardware.

However, the thing we need to keep affirming here is that QR codes shouldn't be overused. Marketers need to realise the simple fact that using them everywhere can be unsafe.

Sometimes, as the scanning process connects two devices together, there is always a high chance of security malfunction.

The user who is scanning usually does not even know about the code and its possibility to take them to an undesignated space of information that they didn't sign up for.

How do QR codes help in marketing?

QR codes give a wide range of prospects to every marketer who is currently looking to diversify or simply find a solid ground to flourish their business.

There are many ways through which QR codes can be used in the marketing sector and utilised in such a way that it boosts the overall growth of a business. Some of them are mentioned in an elucidated manner below-

1. **QR codes can make your business stand out:** QR codes have the ability to generate curiosity among their users, thus aiding a business stand out from its competitors. In order to attract a larger audience, businesses include various offers & QR codes are one of them.
2. **Makes real-life interactions possible:** QR codes add an interactive component by turning static content into dynamic call-to-action buttons. From asking customers to leave a Google review to redirecting them to a branded Facebook page, you have a wide range of options to engage customers.

Let's briefly look at the sectors in which QR codes are utilised.

1. Advertising and marketing
2. Banking account statements
3. Mobile payments
4. HR and payroll
5. Insurance policy
6. Healthcare/lab reports and medical bills
7. Education/university degrees and transcripts

One of the largest applications of QR Codes is in the Paytech or PaymentTech industry. This will be explored in detail in subsequent sections.

5.3. Impediments

No matter how thriving and forward-moving the Fintech industry is, there will always be challenges. And when we are talking about the arising trends, wisdom says that we should also look at the impediments on the way to these evolving trends.

5.3.1 Bridging the Old and the New

Although Fintech has ushered in a technological revolution, it has some significant challenges and issues ahead.

The Fintech industry's trends and digital innovations revolutionised how people, banks, and financial institutions manage their money. Fintech companies continuously build a reputation and enhance their growth in the industry.

Many Fintech companies face setbacks like increasing losses, missed targets, and long-fund-raising cycles. But there are many other issues with Fintech, such as Speed.

While fast transactional speed is one of Fintech's major benefits, it requires companies to adapt various processes. For instance, regulatory and fraud reporting should match this speed. Although some firms can keep up with this expectation, others cannot.

- **Countering Terrorist Financing and Anti-Money Laundering:** These things should be mitigated appropriately. Regulators must share white or black lists for this purpose.
- **Data Privacy:** Inappropriate data usage is another issue that the Fintech industry faces every day, be it payment apps, mobile banking, or technology in general.

Traditional banking systems are confident with heavy bulletproof doors, vaults, CCTVs, and security guards to keep their data safe and secure. But with virtual security, vulnerabilities are more discreet with more impact on users' money and personal data.

- Cross-border Transactions: 'remote services' provision relies on identification and other processes operated in another country.

There are other impediments too, which are as follows:

1. **Cybersecurity:** the use of digital, online banking and payment systems will continue to grow over the next few years. As a result, banks, payment systems, and Fintech providers will need to invest heavily in cybersecurity measures and technologies to ensure the security of their customers' data and financial transactions.

2. **Regulatory Framework:** Banks and Fintech companies must adhere to stringent regulations when it comes to data and financial transactions. As governments become more aware of the potential risks posed by such activities, they may implement stricter regulations in the coming years. This could limit the growth of Fintech companies and their products or services.

3. **Accessibility:** Despite technological progress, many people, especially those in rural or unbanked areas, lack access to financial services, such as online banking or payment systems. This hinders the adoption of Fintech solutions, which are often too complex or costly for these populations.

4. **Data Privacy:** Fintech companies rely on customer data to offer personalised services. However, with the growth of data-driven technologies, customer privacy and data protection concerns are becoming more important than ever before. Fintech companies must comply with increasingly strict data privacy regulations if they want to remain competitive in the future.
5. **Competition:** The rapid growth of Fintech has attracted a growing number of traditional financial institutions, tech giants, and startups into the industry. As competition increases, it could lead to pressure on traditional players to innovate faster or risk losing customers to new entrants who offer better services and products.

Moreover, centralised controls and lack of financial inclusion are two major issues with Fintech that everyone involved in this industry might encounter.

5.3.2 Financial Dinosaurs: Ambling Growth

Most of the old banks are struggling with technology upliftments. Technology backends used in these banks are aged. The majority of the archaic systems were patched in the 1980s, and attempts are being made to integrate them into the newer state-of-the-art systems. Even the cash machines are from the 1990s, causing a lot of non-compliance.

These backend systems are called "Spaghetti systems" because of old solution patches and clumsy integrations with newer systems. This spaghetti leads to major system outages. IT teams are terrified of updating these ancient system applications.

In one instance, the Financial Conduct Authority identified 750,000 customers paying the wrong amount in mortgages – a disaster for those involved.

Bank system costs are mind-blowing. Bank of America allocated $10bn in a single year to modernise its IT, while JP Morgan spent $11.4bn.

But why do banks continue to use outdated software? It is not a matter of desire. Banks make a lot of noise about the need for modernization.

This is where the Dinosaurs' equivalency comes into the picture.

As shown below, there are specific periods defined by Palaeontologists to identify different ages of history.

Similar to the above, the bank's IT teams have to carry out investigative excavations of old financial solutions, as shown below. The details required from older systems are diminishing day by day, but a wrong integration with previous systems is capable of bringing major banking functions.

Modern Systems	2000+	Mobile banking along with ever changing technology demography
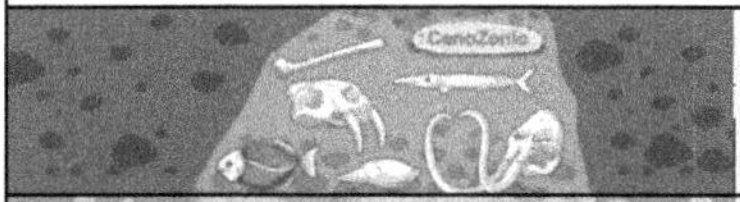 CenoZonic	1980-1990	Phone banking systems deployed integrated with accounting systems. 1994 first internet banking opened (Stanford Federal Credit Union)
 Mesozoic	1960-1970	Cash Machines deployments - Old Card Network integrations with financial systems
 Palaeozoic	1940-1950	Old Credit Systems - Decommissioned Data required for historical purposes

With this approach, IT Teams become equivalent to Palaeontologists. The sheer characteristic of Paleontology is that it takes a long time to do investigations and come up with the outcome.

In a similar way, if banking IT systems have to launch a new product line, they have to adapt to the latest industry standards and work in conjunction with up-to-date technology providers, which in turn integrate with the outdated banking systems. This creates delays because of the old system integrations and security measures. This is the basic reason for the slow growth of the older banks in the modern Fintech ecosystem.

In subsequent sections, we will explore the approaches to mitigate these issues.

5.4. Niche Domains

In February 2016, Abrais - Now "Blueprint Income" Co-Founder Matthew Carey declared the death of Fintech as a Niche sector. He said,

"Financial technology as a niche is dead. No, it's not going away! Rather, financial technology is on the cusp of becoming so entrenched in every aspect of global finance that we'll stop thinking of it as a niche and start thinking of it as the core of how financial services are delivered to consumers, corporations, and institutional investors."

Fintech has effectively transitioned from being a niche domain in the financial services sector to a significant industry with disruptive potential for a variety of reasons, including its independence from legacy systems, simplicity, scalability, customer-centricity, and more.

- **Experts Only Tag**

  Historically, the Fintech domain was established by major financial institutions and was only reserved for experts.

The previous system requires somebody to learn about the financial systems and needs very sound knowledge before entering the domain. This has been a pushed agenda to prevent more and more people from getting into it.

However, it is equally important to break this outdated thought!

With the current technological advancements and many startups entering into Fintech, one can easily access information.

Fintech positions that did not exist a decade ago now play a critical part in all finance jobs. The so-called emerging roles, including machine learning, AI specialists, data analysts, and individuals working in innovation roles, account for about 1 in 7 financial services jobs across The Globe and Mail. This is expected to boom in the coming years.

There is a concern about how Fintech will fill the much-needed positions. Until such time, graduates will hold a high portion of these roles, meeting the needs of the industry, including reskilling the existing staff.

Fintech companies should get more adept at hiring from non-traditional backgrounds. They must focus on areas beyond the financial services industry as well as those outside of the industry.

Technological advancements are the main reason behind Fintech's growth. Since it can operate almost exclusively in a virtual ecosystem, it is now unrecognisable from a decade ago. Algorithms and machines allow automation and cut above traditional financial institutions in different ways, such as more productivity, accessibility, and reduced service fees.

5.5 Complex Processes

Old Fintech employs incredibly antiquated techniques; Now, they are basic.

Technology improvements have made things quick and convenient, so consumers no longer have to wait in lines at banks or fill out a tonne of forms to get loans or other financial services.

Technology has significantly transformed and opened new doors for businesses. The advancements made the Fintech industry eager to stand out by providing improved cross-selling, faster service delivery, and better customer satisfaction to ensure stronger financial health.

Fintech's origins can be traced back to the 1860s. And Fintech can be divided into different eras to highlight its old processes:

1886 – 1967: The first transatlantic cable and Fedwire enabled the first electronic fund transfer system using Morse code and telegraph.

1967 – 2008: In 1967, the first ATM was installed by Barclays Bank, emphasising the digitalization of finances. During the 1970s, the first digital stock exchange, NASDAQ, was established.

1981: Verifone was founded, Verifone has been a pioneer in architecting payments across the global canvas.

1998: PayPal was launched, making the world increasingly online. And in 2008, the global financial crisis prompted innovation in Fintech in the following era.

2008 – Current: In 2009, Bitcoin was introduced, followed by other cryptocurrencies. Smartphone adoption helped people access financial services online.

Today, Fintech automation is a critical factor in simplifying end-to-end financial operations. Many Fintech companies use an enterprise automation platform that controls and runs business events and provides real-time results to automate their processes.

The companies' automation requirements vary. Plus, the IT requirements for automation and integration are different for Fintech. The integration, automation, and growing tech landscape together allow the industry to streamline and accelerate its services.

With integration and automation in Fintech processes, the following innovations are in full swing:

1. Internal process orchestration across SaaS apps

2. Automation strategy and business goals alignment
3. Cloud-based enterprise automation
4. Unified platform for integration and automation
5. Dynamic environments' seamless adaptation
6. Real-time event-driven data operation
7. Agile platforms that enable rapid time-to-deployment
8. More and more Fintech companies choose automation technologies to deliver more seamless and faster services across different digital services.

Summary

- The four main arising bucket trends of Fintech are Communication Systems, Niche Domains, Organised Standards, and Impediments.
- Standardisation of communication is vital in a booming Fintech environment.
- Standards are crucial for the growth of the Fintech industry as it provides a foundation for interoperability, security, and efficiency. Additionally, ensuring that financial transactions are processed correctly and securely. Developing new products and services and expanding into new markets becomes easier for businesses too.
- Some of the most important standards for digital payments include ISO 20022, ISO 8583, and Nexo.
- Next comes the QR codes, which are a type of barcode that can be used for payments. They are becoming highly

popular due to their convenience and security. You just have to scan it on your mobile device and pay. QR codes can be used in a variety of settings, including retail stores, restaurants, and transportation.

- There are two main types of QR codes: static and dynamic. Static codes cannot be modified, while dynamic codes are generated dynamically.
- Coming to the impediments faced by Fintech - data privacy, misuse of data, anti-money laundering, and cybersecurity are some of them.

According to Clayton Christensen, disruptive innovation is the process in which a small player, usually with fewer resources, is able to challenge an established business by entering at the bottom of the market and continuing to move up-market.

Chapter 6

Rapid Disruptions (DAWN)

We had briefly discussed the disruptions in the introductory section of the book. Let us now look at them in a deeper manner. First, let's understand 'Disruptions', a cliched but very significant term.

Disruption means unexpected changes that change existing systems, industries, markets, or patterns of behaviour. Disruptions are caused by technological advancements, shifts in consumer behaviour, regulatory changes, or the introduction of innovative business models.

In the Fintech context, "Rapid Disruptions" have been changing the Fintech ecosystem beyond recognition.

Let us review these rapid disruptions using the key aspects of Dynamic Technology, the App Market, the World Approach and Neo Algorithms.

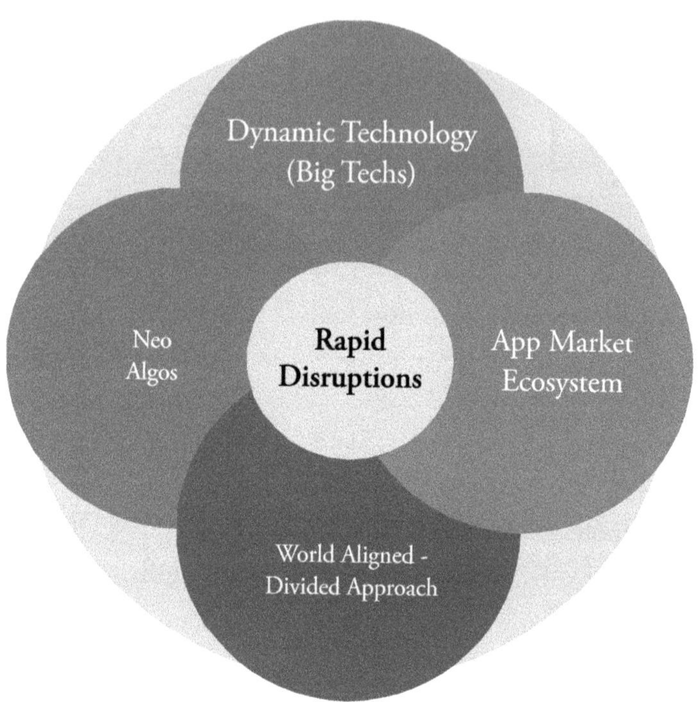

6.1. Dynamic Technology/Big Tech

6.1.1. Big Tech involvement

There are very real reasons for BigTech companies to invest and innovate in Fintech.

1. The overall financial services sector is significant in the growing market. In 2022, the global financial services market was about $25 trillion. This is a substantial opportunity that BigTechs are not going to miss.

2. Fintech is a rapidly growing industry. The Fintech industry is growing at a rate of 20% per year. This growth is being driven by the increasing adoption of mobile devices, the rise of big data, and the growing demand for innovative financial services.
3. BigTechs have the resources to disrupt the financial services industry along with access to vast amounts of data, cutting-edge technology, and deep pockets. This gives them the potential to disrupt the traditional financial services industry, which is often slow to adopt new technologies, as we have seen in earlier sections.
4. Fintech is going to be a fast-track vehicle for BigTech to reach new markets, such as emerging markets and the developing world, because Fintech solutions can be delivered over the internet, which makes them accessible to people in remote areas.

Complementary to the above reasons, there are technological expertise and capability that BigTechs have that can be easily pivoted to deliver Fintech solutions. Some of the key technology areas are as below.

1. **Blockchain:** Blockchain is a distributed ledger technology that can be used to record financial transactions in a secure and transparent way. We will see the details in further sessions.
2. **Artificial intelligence:** AI can be used to automate tasks, personalise financial services, and detect fraud.

3. **Big data:** Big data can be used to analyse financial data and identify trends.

As an outcome of this, we can expect to see even larger tech companies getting involved in Fintech in the coming years.

6.1.2. MAANG

If you follow the financial news, I am sure you would have come across the term MAANG thrown around. Let me assure you it is not a misspelling of an exotic soup.

It's an acronym that stands for five big companies in the high-tech industry that are having a substantial impact on the connected Fintech. It is an acronym of Meta (Facebook), Amazon, Apple, Netflix, and Google.

These American companies have a large global impact. They are household names. Their combined market capitalization exceeds $4 trillion. The blue-chip stocks of the tech sector collectively make up 15% of the Standard & Poor's 500 (an index of the largest public companies in the US). So they represent not only one of the US' most significant industries.

- **Meta/Facebook**

  Facebook Inc. was formed at Harvard in 2004 by Mark Zuckerberg, Eduardo Saverin, Andre McCollum, Dustin Moskovitz, and Chris Hughes. The membership was first restricted to students of Harvard but was later spread to other schools and the rest of the world. Zuckerberg currently owns

WhatsApp, and Instagram, establishing him as the King of all social media. He became the youngest billionaire at 23 and is currently worth around $83 billion.

Facebook Pay was released in 2015 for subscribers in the United States to share money with friends. Unfortunately, the feature did not achieve as much success as Facebook Inc. anticipated, as the social media platform's popularity has waned. WhatsApp, Instagram, and Twitter have surpassed it.

- **Amazon**

  It is the most formidable. If Amazon can get you lower-debt payments or give you a bank account, you'll buy more stuff on Amazon.

  While the anticipation for Amazon's plunge into banking builds each year, it's important to first understand Amazon's existing strategy in financial services — what Amazon has launched and built, where it is investing, and what recent products portray about Amazon's future ambitions.

  Based on our findings, it's hard to claim that Amazon is building the next-generation bank. But it is clear that the company remains very focused on building financial services products that support its core strategic goal: i.e., increasing participation in the Amazon ecosystem.

- **Apple Inc.**

  Apple is an international tech-based firm that was founded by Steve Jobs, Steve Wozniak, and Ronald Wayne back in 1976. The firm produces hardware products that encompass all iOS devices. It is spearheaded by Tim Cook, who was Jobs COO before the latter died in 2011. Tim's current net worth is valued at $1.3 billion.

In 2014, Apple Inc. released the Apple Pay feature that enables all subscribers with an iOS version of 8.1 or higher to make payments and transactions with people who support smartcard transactions.

The feature was initially restricted to customers within the American border but has since spread to over 25 countries, reaching Europe, Africa, Australia, and Asia, while partnering with worldwide reputes like [American Express], Visa and Mastercard to ensure that its global customers can access the payment service irrespective of the type of card they own.

Although the service was launched in 2014, it did not begin to make real strides until 2 years later, when Apple Inc. partnered with Chinese, Australian, French and Canadian financial institutions, with popular businesses like KFC, ExxonMobil Corp. and Starbucks who approved of the feature to make payments.

Between 2017 to the present, the Apple Pay feature has become universal to almost any top businesses in the world, With the feature present on the Apple Watch and mobile devices. Apple Pay also allows iOS users to complete transfers via the use of iMessage.

Apple, on 26 Sep 2022, said it is assembling its flagship iPhone 14 in India as the U.S. technology giant looks to shift some production away from China.Apple's main iPhone assembler, Foxconn, is manufacturing the devices at its

Sriperumbudur factory on the outskirts of Chennai. Apple has been manufacturing iPhones in India since 2017, but these were usually older models. With the iPhone 14, Apple is producing the latest model in its lineup at the device's launch

- **Netflix**

  Netflix is a subscription-based streaming service that allows members to watch TV shows and movies on an internet-connected device. Depending on your plan, you can also download TV shows and movies to your iOS, Android, or Windows 10 device and watch without an internet connection. Netflix has been a pioneer in technological advancements in the streaming industry. It has developed sophisticated recommendation algorithms that customise the content suggestions for users based on their viewing history, preferences. Netflix is one of the first, if not the first big technology company that invested in migrating from the self-hosted environment to AWS - Amazon Web Services' public cloud environment.

  Their application architecture is considered as the reference architecture for distributed microservices software development.

- **Google LLC**

  Google LLC is an international establishment that was set up in 1998 by Larry Page and Sergey Brin, A major subsidiary of a conglomerate known as Alphabet Inc., with the founders' net worth at $66 billion and $62 billion, respectively. Google

LLC launched its Google Pay service in 2018 but has not recorded much success in getting off the ground.

The Google Pay feature is the result of the merger between Google Wallet and Android Pay. The feature is present and functional in 30 countries around the globe.

Once most Android users are fully informed about its availability and operation, it is anticipated to succeed just as well as WeChat Pay and Apple Pay in a few years.

As of 24 Jun 2023: Google to invest $10 billion in India's digitisation fund.

Sunder Pichai said, "We are excited today that we are announcing the opening up of our global fintech operation centre in GIFT city Gujarat,"

6.1.3. BAT

- **Baidu**

  In December 2015, Baidu established a financial services group to enter the consumer finance, mobile payment and internet brokerage businesses. This move was made to compete effectively with other players in the region, such as Alibaba and Tencent, who already have payment services. Since then, the company's financial services business has grown and benefited from its artificial intelligence expertise.

Baidu's AI and big data capabilities can intelligently target and match customers with the right products and identify and prevent fraud. Further, this capability can also assess credit risk through its proprietary data and modelling capabilities. While the company is positioning its financial services business as a Fintech business using technology effectively to differentiate itself, credit rating agencies are considering this to be a high-risk business.

Recently, Fitch placed Baidu on a negative watch as it started moving into unsecured consumer loans and uninsured investments, which are considered to be riskier and "part of the shadow banking system" in China.

While Search Services still remain the most valuable segment for Baidu (accounting for more than 60% of its valuation, according to our estimates), the company is diversifying into several other areas to leverage its AI capabilities. Further, after stricter regulations, advertising on search engines is now controlled, leading to lower revenues for Baidu. Financial Services is a growth area for Baidu, and the company needs to expand in this segment to stay competitive with players such as Alibaba and Tencent.

China's financial industry is growing at an exponential pace, and there is demand for a more inclusive finance system. A large population of the country falls in the lower income category and does not meet the criteria laid out by many banks for credit products. This gap is being filled by technology giants such as Baidu, who are using big data and artificial intelligence to determine the creditworthiness of individuals. While there is certainly demand for this, it is a high-risk business. While Baidu believes that its AI capabilities can help manage the credit risk of consumers, the company needs to tread carefully on this path.

Baidu already faced a significant reputation loss when misleading medical advertisements on its platform contributed to the death of a college student. This impacted its search business negatively, and the company needs to ensure that its financing arm does not run into any trouble as it extends unsecured loans. Baidu's financial services group now accounts for nearly 12% of its total assets, and the company is looking to expand this segment to capture the opportunities in this space. While the current Fitch downgrade does not put Baidu in the non-investment grade category, the company is likely to tread carefully in this space to avoid any issues.

- **Ant Financial Services Group**

  This is an online payment platform established in 2004 in China by Jack Ma and the Alibaba group. For the first 10 years of the startup, the business was known as Alipay but is now known as Ant Financial. As of right now, the firm is the biggest pure TechFin establishment in the world today, valued at around $150 billion. In 2013, the firm was announced to edge out PayPal as the biggest online payment service on the globe. By 2016, the firm had over 400 million active subscribers worldwide, But the number has since neared 1 billion subscribers by 2020. In 2017, the firm proposed to acquire MoneyGram as a subsidiary for a fee in the region of $900 million, but the deal was unable to fall through due to some American security issues. In the same year, the firm released the facial recognition feature for payment options.

  By 2018, the firm established a direct money-wiring service

option between the Philippines and China. Then it went on to set a record for the highest amount ever raised in a single day, with the funds totalling nearly $15 billion. In 2019, the firm bought World First Ltd. for a sum of over $690 million. Later, it went on to partner up with Barclays to ensure that Chinese expatriates in the United Kingdom can have easy payment options through their stay in the UK. Currently, the firm's Alipay operates in over 50 nations around the world while partnering with worldwide reputations like VISA and MasterCard to ensure that its global customers can access the payment service regardless of the type of card they own.

- **Tencent WeChat**

  Tencent WeChat is a China-based tech establishment, launched in 2011 and started as a social media messaging system but now has a mobile transaction service used for citizen monitoring throughout China. The service is one of the biggest mobile applications, boasting of a monthly mean of one billion users. The service was initially known as Weixin but was swapped for WeChat when it reached a century of millions of subscribers. The transaction service was released 2 years after its initial launch, and by 2016, recorded over 350 million people using the payment service "WeChat Pay". It requires all subscribers to link the account to their credit cards. The transaction is immediate for all Chinese subscribers however requires extra identity certification of all non-Chinese users before transactions can be completed. On the last day of January 2014, WeChat Inc. added a "red envelope" attribute to the payment service for monetary gift-giving to a selected group of people. The attribute consists of two forms, in which the funds can be paid evenly or at random, depending on whichever the subscriber chooses. By 2016, over 3 billion "red envelopes" had been sent out, with over 400,000 on February 8th. As of right now, WeChat Pay has surpassed AliPay to become the largest online payment service in China, with a lot of its subscribers from its huge social media database.

6.1.4. Startup Ecosystem

Fintech landscape continuously evolves, and we expect the newest developments.

According to McKinsey Panorama, almost 80% of financial institutions have entered Fintech partnerships. Meanwhile, in 2018, the global venture capital Fintech investment already reached $30.8 billion.

A long time ago, a transfer of values occurred between commoners, merchants, and royalty who used cattle, silver, gold, and other physical commodities to survive.

But in the past years, Fintech has become a global phenomenon and game-changer in the financial services sector. Fintech has grown dramatically across business lines and geographies. It has the ability to develop and deliver innovative products in real-time, provide better value and convenience to customers, and address issues not properly solved by traditional financing.

Listed below are the ways and ideas that have shaken up the Fintech ecosystem is shaken with new thoughts and new inventions:

- The growth of Fintech across geographies and products.
- The proliferation of Fintech startups across all geographies, particularly in the UK, USA, and China.
- The entry of Fintech in major business lines of financial services, such as wealth management, savings, transfers, lending, and payments.
- The rise and consolidation of Fintech champions.
- Successful Fintech companies' consolidation, which attracts more investments.
- Partnerships and acquisitions with other Fintech players.
- The new product launches helped complement the businesses' service portfolio.
- The Introduction of banking-as-a-service.
- A new platform to match the financial service providers with customers.
- The forging partnerships between established organisations and Fintech potentially disrupt the financial service sector.
- The banking regulation evolution fosters data use and future partnerships.
- The evolution of banking-as-a-service.
- AI usage to cluster the same customers and deliver customised offers by predicting the most relevant financial services.
- The combination of financial services from various providers to develop bundles.

6.2. The App Market Ecosystem

In this section, we will understand the App Market ecosystem. As all the day-to-day activities, be it finance, shopping, banking etc.. are available on mobile apps, it is imperative to understand where we are in terms of the availability of these apps and how the world of mobile phones changing the behavioural patterns of consumers.

6.2.1. Mobile Device Availability

In 2022, the global forecast is that the world population would reach 8 billion. Now let us look at important statistics regarding the usage of mobile phones by this global population.

The figure below will give you a perfect idea of the stupendous growth in the volume of mobile phones year on year.

As you can see, the sheer number of mobile phones in the world is almost double that of the population, indicating two mobile phones per user. This is an important factor denoting access to technology and, essentially, Fintech from mobile phones.

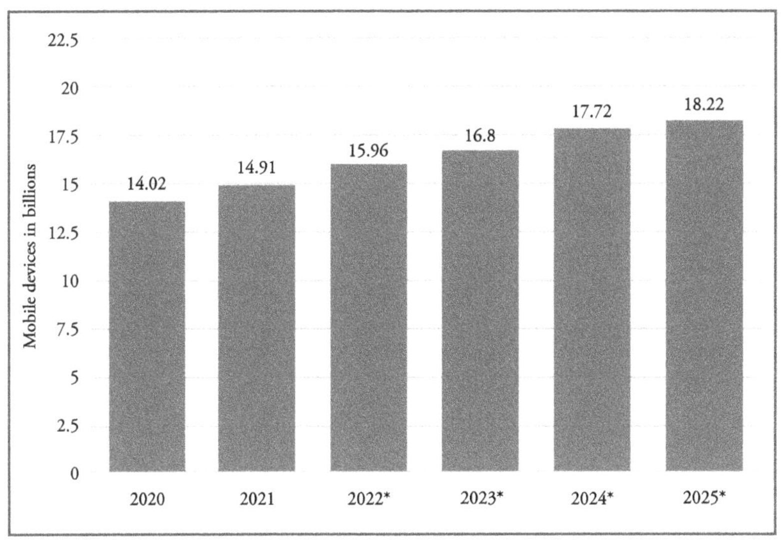

Number of mobile devices worldwide 2020-2025, Statista

Each of us is using mobile phones for much more than sending and receiving calls or messages. The amount of smartphones in the world is reaching 40% of the overall number of mobile phones. This smartphone usage is increasing at a very fast rate. We have a complete ecosystem based on data exchange.

The following statistics depicted in the figure below show monthly data usage year on year.

We are looking at 83 Exabytes of monthly data usage in the year 2022, increasing to three times in the next five years.

83 Exabytes meaning 83 million TeraBytes (1 exabyte = 1,000,000 terabytes). This is a staggering data usage indicating a large amount of App usage.

Also, the more functionalities Apps provide, the higher the prices they would attract. With the technological development of In-App, a specific function or feature can be used for a while with additional cost. All these applications increase the financial worth of the companies developing as well as hosting these apps in their specific mobile marketplace.

Though Apps have regional flavours in their behaviour, at the same time, monetization is their common underlying goal. Every region and country has a specific payment processing model to support mobile Apps. Each day, more and more Fintechs are tapping into this ecosystem.

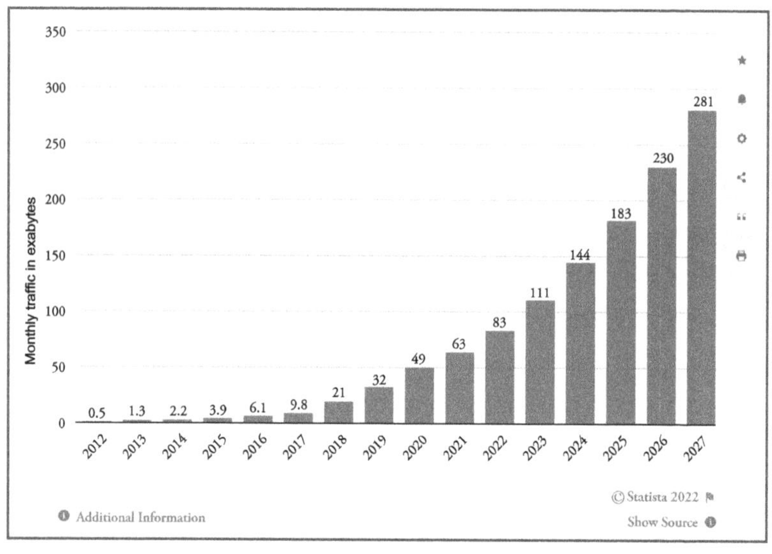

Average monthly smartphone traffic worldwide 2027, Statista

Till this point in time, we are looking at Apps in general, but with the advent of multiple Fintech companies related to banking, loans, insurance and even cryptocurrencies, Fintech is available to the end consumer at their fingertips using mobile phones.

6.2.2. App Developers

The charts in the figure below will prove to be an eye-opener for the huge potential of startups in the App development landscape.

The sheer number of apps is in millions. The AppMarket has a large contribution to the bottom line of these companies, with Apple's revenue projection at 360 BN USD and Alphabet's (Google) around 260 BN USD for 2022.

According to the Statista website, the Q2 2022 number of applications on Android and Apple's iOS are as follows.

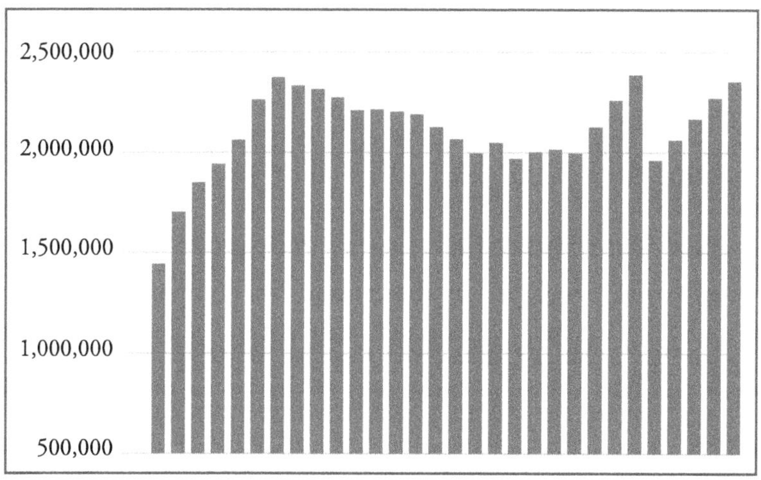

Apple's iPhone Apps by Q2 2022: 2.2 million worldwide

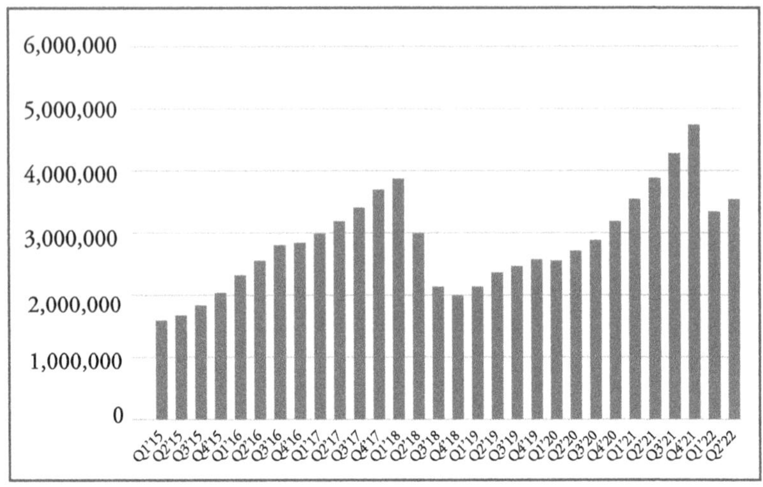

Android Apps by Q2 2022: 3.5 million worldwide

Apple's iPhone Apps by Q2 2022: 2.2 million worldwide
Android Apps by Q2 2022: 3.5 million worldwide.

Now, these Apple iOS apps - 2.2 MN and Android 3.5 MN are not at all developed by these respective companies. They are providing a marketplace where third parties can develop their Apps and host them for consumers to download on their mobile phones.

According to industry experts, there are approximately 6 Million android developers worldwide who build applications for the Android phone market (around 82% of the smartphone market). As for Apple's iOS - there are estimated 2.8 million iOS developers worldwide for Apple Phones (approx 18% of the smartphone market).

6.2.3. Taking Finance to the Consumer

With the above data & diagrams, we have understood the overall smartphone market, its usage and the development community.

The numbers are staggering and being leveraged by the industry to reach every mobile phone user.

The largest footprint of the applications used on a daily basis other than social media are online shopping applications.

Nearly 35% of millennials consider the Amazon Mobile App as the most essential app.

The Mobile App industry revenue is projected to be around USD 935 billion dollars by 2023 (source: Statista).

[This is only from paid app downloads on in-app advertising and not by actually using apps for purchasing.]

55+ Jaw-Dropping App Usage Statistics in 2022 [Infographic] (techjury.net)

- Total 175 billion App downloads per year
- Average number of Apps on a smartphone is 80
- Average user uses 9 Apps daily and 30 Apps monthly

6.2.4 Fintech Apps

Till now, we were talking about Apps in general now let's look at Fintech Apps in particular.

- Fintech applications are used for multiple business cases such as, but not limited to personal finance,

- Investment,
- Crowdfunding,
- Money Lending,
- Savings,
- Money Transfer, and
- Lending etc.

Fintech applications were created by financial institutions, tech giants and also financial startups complementing the marketplace as per the needs

One of the highest growing industries, India has the second-highest penetration rate for Fintech goods in the country, at 59 per cent.

The broad categories of core Fintech Apps globally are as follows. This does not include the standard applications where payments are offered. These are Fintech services apps only. The categories are as follows, and we can dive into the details as required.

1. Internet Banking
2. Digital Wallets & Digital Payments
3. Wealth Portfolio Management
4. Market Investments - Stocks Trading/Mutual funds/IPOs
5. Crypto Trading

6.3. World Aligned- Divided Approach

We have already discussed details about technology companies and also the App market ecosystem and how that is greatly influencing the Fintech industry globally. One thing is becoming clear by 2020, the world realised that Fintech apps are here to stay.

However, this brings us to a question:

Does this mean that the same app would work across the world?

6.3.1. Fintech Global Alignment

There is no straight answer to this question - we need to consider the following constraints for applying Fintech use cases for a country or region.

These constraints are aligned with the mobile app categories defined in earlier sessions as the categories are the same across the world, i.e. there is an alignment of connected Fintech services categories from the consumer perspective.

The following table illustrates this in a simple manner.

#	Global Fintech App Category	Typical Fintech Services Offered
1	Internet Banking	Account balance, statements. Fund transfers. Tax payments. Bank investment instruments like fixed deposits
2	Digital Wallets & Digital Payments	Peer to Peer Payments, Bill Payments
3	Wealth Portfolio Management	Asset and expenses tracking - growth recommendations and projections
4	Market Investments - Stocks Trading/Mutual funds/IPOs	Stock trading - Buy/Sell stocks, mutual funds. Invest in IPOs
5	Crypto Trading/ NFT	Crypto Currency buying and selling. NFT digital assets management

6.3.2. Different Approaches

As we have established the fact that the Fintech services provided globally are in alignment, the apps, however, are different regionally.

That brings us to a logical question:

Why do we have the same service provided in different regions and ways?

Why can't it be similar to an email or a cloud storage provider where the service offered is uniform?

Fintech is a very critical industry based on the law of the land.

Every region/country has their own currency issued by respective central banks governed by standard regulatory industries.

Fintech services are also regulated in accordance with this.

There are specific aspects of KYC (Know your customer), Central Bank regulations on funds transfer, unique government ID like an Aadhaar Number (issued by Unique Identification Authority of India), Social Security Number and corresponding authentication process - a biometric or OTP (One Time Password).

It is because of these region/country-specific aspects, along with other data retention and data protection regulations, that the applications and the application developers are different across the regions/countries.

Keeping this in mind, let us look at what are the top applications in specific regions/countries globally.

#	Global Fintech App Category	India	United States	Europe	United Kingdom
1	Internet Banking	- SBI Yono - ICICI iMobile	- Capital One App - Bank of America	- N26 Neo Bank - Germany - Eurobank App	- Starling App - Barclays Bank App
2	Digital Wallets & Digital Payments	- PayTM - GooglePay - BHIM	- Zelle - Paypal/ Venmo	- MobilePay - Skrill	- ApplePay
3	Wealth Portfolio Management	- IND Money	- Personal Capital	- Dorsum	

4	Market Investments - Stocks Trading/Mutual funds/ IPOs	- Zerodha	- Etrade	- XTB online trading	- IG UK
5	Crypto Trading / NFT	- WazirX	- Coinbase	- FTX	- Binance

(Source: Multiple Websites)

* Standard applications like ApplePay, GooglePay, Paypal are globally widely used for payments.

AliPay and WeChatPay which are also accepted worldwide are issued by China-based conglomerate Alibaba and Tencent respectively.

** Standard portfolio tools like Yahoo Money, Google Finance are top applications globally available for the majority of the markets.

6.4. Neo Algos

Life & business today are so dynamic that almost every day, there are new algorithms being introduced into every space, and Fintech is no exception to this. New algorithms increasingly impact decision-making. And this affects people's lives, including how they engage with the financial services space.

Spending data, consumer data, and other data describing people's behaviour are excellent sources of information necessary for developing financial services. Additionally, natural language processing and computer imaging advances enable data augmentation to develop exciting fresh propositions.

Machine learning algorithms have become more powerful at personalising and categorising information. They also help identify anomalies. The availability of data from countless sources is surging, which is enabled by APIs, Big Data, and the Internet of Things.

Let us explore these arising trends below individually.

- **Blockchain**

Blockchain is expected to disrupt established financial protocols.

With distributed ledger technology (DLT), recording and sharing of data across data stores is possible. It also allows recording, sharing, and synchronisation of transactions and data across a distributed network.

Blockchain is used by some DTLs to transmit and store data. The DTL increasingly underpins ecosystem financing through financial transactions storage in multiple places at once. Technologies such as zero-knowledge proof, smart contracts, and distributed data exchange and storage are critical to the existing Fintech innovations, like non-fungible tokens (NFTs), decentralised finance (DeFi), digital assets, and digital wallets.

Other blockchain applications include:

- Real-time transaction settlement

- Digital asset support services
- Authenticating ecosystem according to zero-knowledge proof
- Decentralised Finance
- AI/ML
- Artificial intelligence (AI) and machine learning (ML) continuously expand in applications, scope, and importance in Fintech sector, including:
- Better and stronger security
- Improved customer service
- Intelligently designed financial apps
- Enhanced algorithm trading and decision-making
- Increased productivity with low resources
- Improved fraud detection
- Automated credit, loan approval, and risk assessment
- The incredible potential of AI in Fintech is now becoming apparent. Almost all aspects of the modern digital world utilise AI and ML. Every upgrade allows AI systems to be more reliable and powerful.

- **RPA**

Robotic Process Automation (RPA) has a critical role in Fintech. Different sectors, including Fintech, use robots to automate their processes and activities. This improves operational productivity while reducing overall costs. Companies and institutions that offer financial services make their work easier and quicker by taking recourse to software technology, cloud services, mobile devices, etc.

People increasingly turn digital in their actions and mindsets. They want to obtain loans, transfer funds, make payments, or invest money as quickly as possible using hassle-free methods.

And RPA is highly useful here as it:

- Improves customer service
- Enhances productivity
- Improved the accounting process
- Improves investments
- The union of technology and financial services resulted in rapid disruptions. More and more financial institutions are engaged with Fintech startups through strategic partnerships or as investors.

Disrupting Fintech Industry:

1. **Open Banking:** Open banking is a disruptive force in the financial technology space as it allows customers to share their financial data with third-party service providers. It enables customers to access services through the use of application programming interfaces (APIs) that allow them to securely share their financial data with other providers and companies.
2. **Digital Wallets:** Digital wallets are another disruption that has taken the Fintech world by storm. These wallets allow customers to store and use their payment information

digitally, often through mobile devices, eliminating the need for debit cards and cash. This not only offers more convenience for customers but also enhanced security against fraud as data is encrypted at all times.

3. **Digital Currencies:** Cryptocurrencies have also been a major source of disruption in the Fintech world. Bitcoin, the most popular example, has enabled users to transfer funds quickly and securely without having to rely on third-party intermediaries like banks or credit card companies. This has provided a level of financial freedom and anonymity that can be hard to find in traditional banking options.

4. **Investment Apps:** Investment apps are also playing a major role in disrupting the Fintech world by allowing users to invest without the need for a broker or financial advisor. They provide an accessible way for users to access the stock market, as well as providing educational resources to help them make informed investing decisions.

Summary

- Big tech companies are greatly involved in the Fintech industry; some top ones among them are FAAN companies (Facebook, Apple, Alphabet and Netflix) The prime factor is the technological expertise that these Bigtechs bring (blockchain, artificial intelligence and big data), is leading to the success of Fintech.
- Big tech companies have helped in areas such as launching payment systems, offering lending products and investment

services. Additionally, they have the advantage of having a bigger proportion of users, access to data, and innovative ways. The entry of Big Tech companies in Fintech is set to usher in the end of the traditional financial services industry.

- Fintech has hit the mark in developing and delivering unique products that excel in serving customer needs at a fairer value. The ecosystem of Fintech has gone beyond geographies and business lines, stepping into an era of the evolution of banking as a service.
- Exploring the App market ecosystem data reveals that the use of mobile phones in the world has doubled in recent times. As more and more people have access to mobile phones, banking and financial services are becoming easier to use on our mobile devices through apps. Therefore, the expansion of Fintech is shaped by the widespread accessibility of mobile technology.
- A number of new technologies, including neo algos, blockchain, AI/ML, and RPA, are disrupting the Fintech industry, thereby aiding the industry to stride into the future with improved customer service, automated processes, and secured financial transactions.

By watching each step today, we pave a path to a better future.

Chapter 7

Now and Futures (The 5Ds of Fintech)

In the preceding sections, we have gone through all the aspects of Fintech that, includes the Evolution, Arising Trends, and Rapid Disruptions.

After careful consideration, it is evident that Fintech domains are stretched across various industries and demand a consistent model to drive this initiative forward.

So what exactly is a model?

A model is typically a simplified representation of a complex ecosystem.

This means that the model may not include all of the details of the real thing, however, it does include the critical concepts that describe the ecosystem with specific constraints and guidelines.

Models are often used to extrapolate and forecast the trajectory of the specific domain system.

These are representations of real-world problems and very useful tools for understanding how things work.

Here I am sharing with you the 5Ds Fintech model provides a set of best practices that organisations can consider to build Fintech solutions.

The 5D model can be used to:

- Identify the technology transitions that are happening in the behaviour of the Fintech marketplace
- Assess the impact of change on the user behaviour
- Build a plan to accommodate the behaviour and technology together
- 5D is a valuable tool for anyone who is involved in Fintech. It is simple to use and can be applied to all Fintech solutions.

The diagram below illustrates the concept and application of the 5Ds of Fintech, with each of them being discussed in detail.

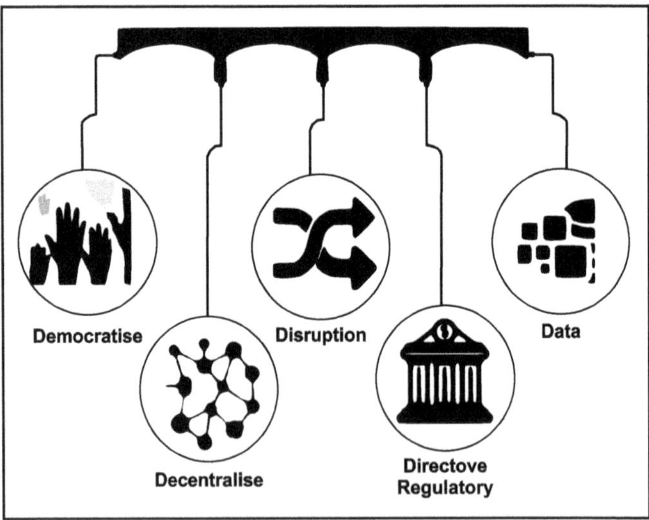

The 5Ds are:

1. **Democratisation of Finance:** Refers to the optimum utilisation of underused assets. Also, making sure the financial services are available to a wider range of consumers using easy-to-use apps and websites.
2. **Decentralisation of Finance** can completely turn the global economy on its head by making the finance sector transparent and more easily accessible. With the advent of the new technological advancements of blockchain, this has become a reality.
3. **Disruptions**, as seen in earlier sections of the EARN model, are new patterns & algorithms in the Fintech domains- Rapid disruptions were already reviewed in detail earlier. The trend continues, and we will review the newer disruptions in the industry.
4. **Directive Regulatory:** With technological advancement, new risks are manifested, and there is a need for strict monitoring & regulation. The regulatory bodies drive and build the compliance models to mitigate the risks that include cybersecurity, fraud etc.
5. **Data-Driven:** The major reason for the efficient use of any system is the transparency and the feedback loop from the system. The Data Generated out of the modern Fintech ecosystems is the latest currency. We will look into the details of modelling this data.

Let us dig deeper & build our knowledge base on each of these individual Ds of the 5D model.

Sharing assets is like spreading goodness, the more we spread the better society becomes.

Chapter 8

Democratised Finance

We all are aware of democracy, especially in the terms of the visionary Abraham Lincoln-

Of the people,
By the people
and For the people.

Today the industry is striving to democratise technology platforms to cater to a wider consumer base as well as to provide services that were not possible before because the right information at the right time was inaccessible.

Fintech is a very crucial component of this democratisation as both suppliers and users must be paid, and the platform must be sustained to provide better services.

The diagram below explains in great detail and very clearly the 'Democratisation of Finance' with every component basis the democratic concept of - Of, For & By the people.

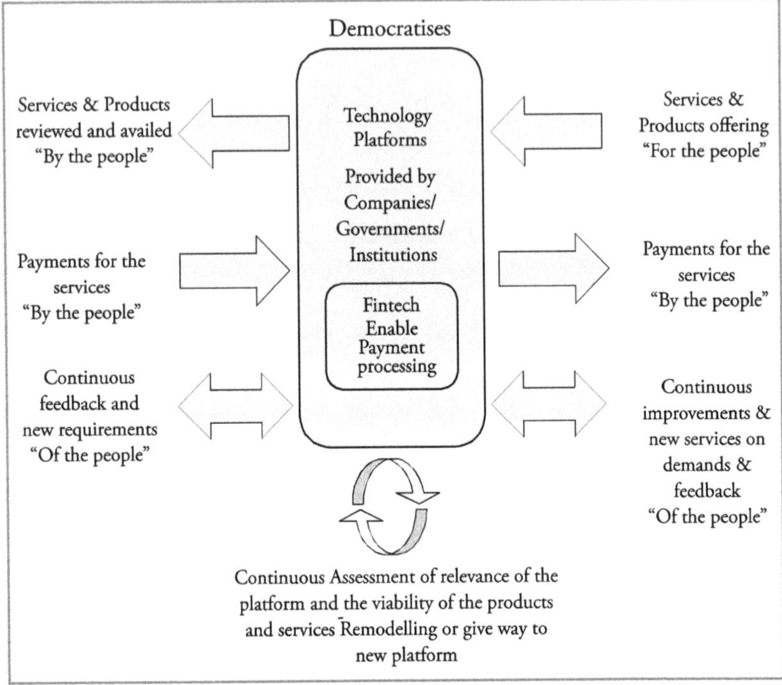

8.1. The 5G Evolution Enabling Revolution in Fintech Offerings

Today, the majority of us have started to use 5G technology from our phones, tablets and laptops.

But is 5G easily available to everyone globally in every nook and corner of the world?

The straightforward answer is - no!

But at the same time, multiple providers are launching 5G services, and in due course of time, 5G services would be accessible to everyone.

The other factor is the availability of the 5G hardware and 5 G-compliant operating systems.

It will take at least the next couple of years to replace all the existing devices with the new 5G devices.

This raises a vital question -

Is the 5G technology a Revolution or an Evolution?

According to Forbes magazine, 5G technology is an evolution which will gradually change the app ecosystem and services. 5G is an evolution as it builds on existing progress in both telecommunications and banking.

5G technology is backwards compatible, which means 5G phones "are capable of functioning on earlier-generation networks outside of 5G coverage areas". **This enables the providers to continue to maintain 4G networks as they build 5G networks.**

Fintech innovations are already deemphasizing "brick and mortar" financial transactions. The need has only increased during the pandemic. A significant number of Fintechs are now focused on building a touchless, safe, fast and easy-to-use customer experience. 5G will help make these features ubiquitous, particularly in rural areas.

Then why are we saying that the 5G evolution is enabling the Fintech revolution?

The explanation is rather simple- Behind any revolution, there is always a trigger. This 5G evolution is acting as a trigger for the Fintech revolution.

M2M (Machine to Machine data exchange) communication had some restrictions - because of the limited 4G bandwidth, the apps developed were with a limited data exchange capability.

These restrictions can be considered obsolete with the advent of the 5G.

However, this does not apply to all the applications as the standard applications continue to function as they are in a more "backwards compatible" mode.

At the same time, Fintech is ready to embrace 5G for the new revolutionary Apps that could not be thought of prior to 4G.

This means that although the technology is evolutionary, i.e. the telecommunication bandwidth is widening, enabling Fintech companies to develop new Apps that could actually consume this substantially wider bandwidth.

Typical examples are:

1. **Fintech service personalisation:** A personalised financial service experience when interacting with increasingly data-laden offerings and connected by APIs to various other data sources is now available even if the consumer is travelling on high-speed trains.

   This will drastically eliminate the cost and efforts of customer acquisition for Sintech services as well as the provisioning of VR Agents and chatbot advisors on mobiles. This will soon be available flawlessly to the users of 5G networks.

2. **Fintech IoT:** 5G's primary use case is in connecting more devices at lower power and cost, with more reliability. As a result, the advent of 5G is expected to be met with a surge in Internet of Things (IoT) devices, including smartphones, wearables, home appliances and public infrastructure.

   This will offer banks and payment providers further ground to innovate, making payments more seamless between devices and sensors and services a natural and secure part of their customers' daily activities when combined with wearables, AR and biometrics. A customer could use a pair of augmented reality smart glasses to scan a product for sale in a store, apply a discount code and purchase instantaneously, aim their smartphone at a concert poster and buy their ticket with a single swipe or nod of the head. Only 5G bandwidth will be able to support these intricate solutions, which would revolutionise Fintech Marketplace.

3. **Stock trading Transformation:** A new age of high-frequency trading that will revolutionise stock market transactions may likewise be brought about by 5G.

As per leading economic advisors, it will be possible for complex decision-making AI/ML models, such as those related to politics, economics, society and technology to be taken into consideration in real-time to achieve intelligent trading analysis and make decisions basis the analysis.

With the success of buying and selling – and millions of dollars per year – coming down to in just split seconds, 5G will be a highly-attractive technology for brokerage firms, who will be some of the most eager adopters.

This would involve drawing insights from social media: "Virtual Brokers on mobile devices enable securities trading anywhere and anytime. These brokers are practically avatars which are implemented with VR and Natural Language Processing technologies. One of the possibilities of using sophisticated AI algorithms would be that a broker can read facial expressions and understand the conversations of the clients. Based on that, it can recommend the best investment tactics to the consumer.

Essentially 5G will transform Fintech into new possibilities democratising finance, bringing digitally-savvy customers novel and revolutionary services like never before.

8.2. Sharing Economy - Sharing Fintech

Since the last ten years, the "Sharing Economy" has been a diversification of commerce with a new shared resource structure. Startups Like Airbnb, UBER, Lyft, Ola, Oyo, and Yulu hit the market, providing collaborative consumption, peer-to-peer needs, and sharing of an underutilised asset.

Business models can be built on collaboration, sharing, and an entity availability model like partial sharing. In every aspect, the definition is constructive for the sharing economy.

We all have heard of the following revolutionary statement:

"Uber, the world's largest taxi company, owns no vehicles. Facebook, the world's most popular media owner, creates no content. Alibaba, the most valuable retailer, has no inventory. And Airbnb, the world's largest accommodation provider, owns no real estate."

Though this statement sounds impossible, the truth is that it has been made possible by the disruption of the 'shared economy model' enabled solely by technology.

Let's deconstruct this model a bit more to understand why these business economies arise.

We are living in a world where resources are limited; consumption is very sporadic and inconsistent. We see a lot of available resources, but they are limited to a certain section of consumers.

Therefore, proper utilisation of adequate assets to meet every user's demand must be executed. With the growing demand for undervalued products, we need a proper institutional framework which allocates equitable distribution of resources.

A great disruption has been enabled with technology working as a backbone for modelling business behaviour along with user-friendly interfaces - Apps to optimise the usage of these undervalued resources.

The Diagonal Shift of Capital Investment in the Sharing Economy based startup is in surplus YoY.

Listed below are the key aspects of the Sharing Economy:

1. **Tech Explosion:** Globally integrated Digital Payment adoption along with robust software enhancement led to mass acceptance of technology using mobile Apps. Multiple business models - usage-based, resource-based and location-based define the service offering at the right place and right price.
2. **Value Against Assets:** A connected society with a large agnostic, young, tech-aware population is using a value-based approach rather than an emphasis on asset creation. The services being offered are changing based on the need of the hour and the location. Therefore, there is a lot of rethinking going on into what ownership provides, in contrast to the value of sharing in the digital age.
3. **Growth Story - Revenue Models:** This refers to the growing realisation that we need to think about wealth and assets through a new perspective and measure 'growth' in a more meaningful way. This realisation is breaking down the conventional models of assets and ownership. Businesses are also thinking of offering more services than selling one-time products. The revenue models are more focused on recurring revenues.
4. **Environmental Utilisation:** With ever-growing climate concerns and the preservation of natural resources - the world has realised that the resources are limited, and we

need to make optimum use of the available resources to avoid a situation where we are left with no resources at all.

5. **Community Platforms:** This is a path-breaking concept that is enabled due to the technology and Fintech evolution. These community platforms provide global citizens with a common place to avail a specific service. The service providers and consumers both use this platform.

Essentially, this platform connects the global communities of service providers and consumers to offer a service at the right place and price. Fintech plays a very crucial role in these community platforms as these services are required to be paid by consumers in the payment mode and currency accepted by the service provided based on their location. Fintech eases this by bridging the gap and offering multiple options, hiding the complexity of the payment transfer from one currency to another and from the consumer's account to the service provider's account.

These aspects have given rise to the companies like Airbnb and OLA.

The figure below details a typical model of the Sharing-Economy, explaining in detail how the technology-enabled interface works to connect consumers and service providers to make optimal use of shared resources.

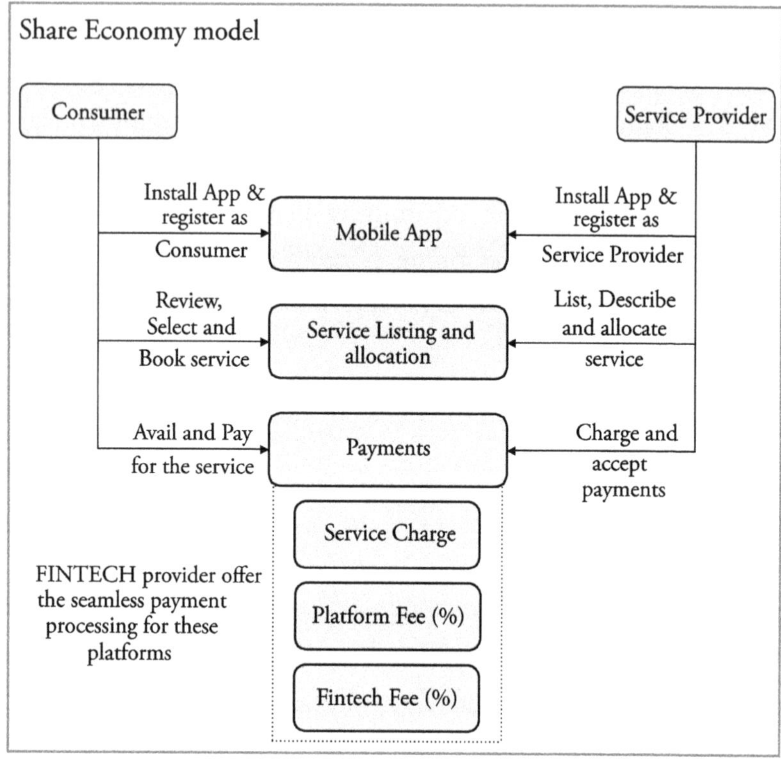

As is clear, the above schematic explains the connection between the consumer and service provider using the Fintech stack. The primary intersection points are the services listed and the payment mode offered to the consumer.

Today this is available in dedicated Afor specific services like booking shared accommodation on holiday or booking a taxi.

This can also be available as part of a Super App that we will talk about later in the book.

8.2.1. Sharing Economy Companies - AirBNB

To give you a better idea of how the sharing economy works, let's apply this model to deconstruct how the AirBNB system works- similarly, it can be applied to all the Sharing economy - community platforms.

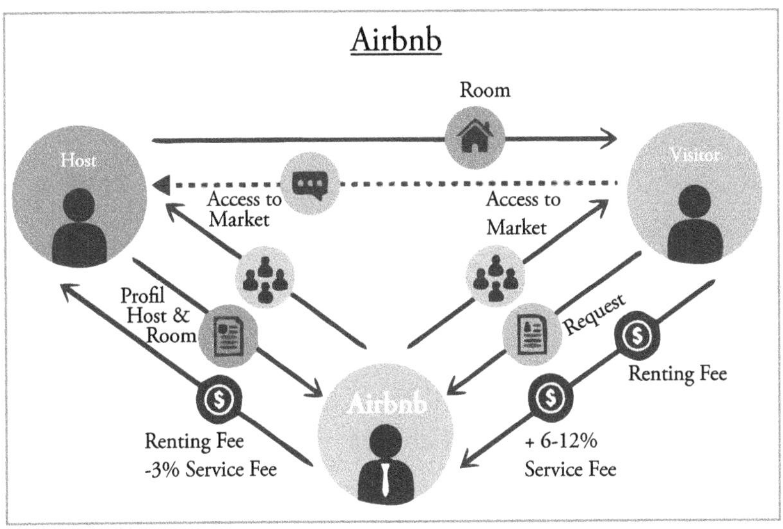

Source: bmtoolbox.net

8.2.2. Global Sharing Economy Companies

Please refer to the analysis detailed in the figure below, done by PWC on sharing economy performance, and you will be amazed to see how the shared economy has taken a leap from a mere 5 % in 2012 to a projected massive 50 % in 2025. That's an unbelievable disruption indeed.

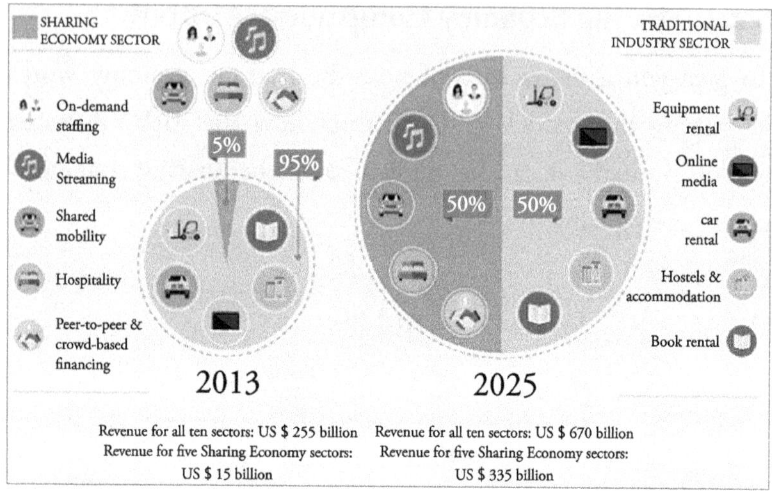

Illustrative revenue potential across five traditional and Sharing Economy sectors; Source: PWC - The Sharing Economy.

An estimated $23bn in venture capital funding was poured into the market between 2010 and 2017, according to a report by the Boston Consulting Group.

Now there are thousands of sharing economy companies riding the wave of this profitable trend. For your reference and understanding, I am sharing below a list of the top sharing economy companies in the world.

8.3. Lend-Tech - Loans and Microfinance

Lend-Tech is a Fintech domain for providing loans and other financial assistance services to the right consumer in a secure environment. As the term indicates, these are digital platforms for banks and other financial loaning institutions to provide loans. These loans can be in multiple categories and with specific constraints.

The categories typically include:

1. Institution-to-Institution lending
2. Institution to consumer lending
3. Peer-to-Peer lending
4. Microfinance/Microlending

Lending is one of the primary functions of financial institutions if not the biggest function. Fintech has enhanced and extended the capability of these financial institutions (FIs) to provide an efficient way of lending. Lending is essentially the function of creating credit to drive development in the world. This has always been the case. Credit enables institutions and consumers to borrow money that they do not have at that point in time, thereby executing projects which they would not be able to do otherwise.

As examples of the typical lending categories listed above, these are, for instance, the loans taken by governments for building the infrastructure of the country like bridges, public buildings, sports complexes, transport infrastructure etc.

As far as standard home loans or mortgage loans are considered, they allow consumers to buy properties and then repay over multiple years as agreed with the lender. If these credits did not exist, it would have become very difficult for governments and consumers to build infrastructures.

Similarly, automobile loans or car leases are other common types of loans. Additionally, FIs also provide personal loans that consumers can avail of for any incidental purposes.

The important aspect of lending money is to have strict criteria. In the aftermath of the 2008 global financial crisis, FIs have been very diligent and downright stringent while approving any type of loan.

If the creditworthiness of the applicant, whether it is an institution or consumer, is not appropriate enough, FI simply denies access to finances.

Till a few years ago, till the late 1990s, getting rejected from FIs would force the consumer to only go to "Loan Sharks". However, the advent of Fintech enables better access to finances because of the multi-level credit checking and verifying credit worthiness. This has been reasonably successful in reducing the Loan Shark parallel economy that hurts consumers.

According to Wikipedia, "A loan shark is a person who offers loans at extremely high interest rates, has strict terms of collection upon failure, and generally operates outside the law. Because loan sharks operating illegally cannot reasonably expect to be able to use the legal system to collect such debts, they often resort to enforcing repayment by blackmail and threats of violence."

Peer-to-Peer lending, business-to-customer and business-to-business lending platforms have become an industry on their own in the last ten years. According to estimates, the Fintech lending industry will be worth over $390 billion by 2023.

8.3.1. The Lend-Tech Model Platform

Here, let us focus on the Fintech lending model and platform.

This will enable us to focus more on marketplace lending rather than institution-to-institution lending.

Typically lending platforms may not only utilise standard Financial institutions but also add investors/donors, thus connecting lenders and borrowers on this common virtual marketplace.

Lenders register with the platform and invest their funds. These Fintech lending platforms have their own set of terms and conditions and also come with their individual set of risks. Based on the risk appetite of the investors, they can choose the platform suited to them. A general thumb rule is- the higher the risk higher the returns.

Refer to the model shown in the diagram below, which connects borrowers and consumers with financial institutions. The schematic shows the typical functional stack of the Lendtech platform. This image gives complete insight into the steps of issuing a loan and tracking the payments from the borrower over the tenure of the loan.

Borrowers are connected with lenders on these platforms. Essentially the lend-tech platform keeps the lender at the backend and manages the borrowers on the front end.

This is how many Fintech lending platforms work.

- Borrowers register themselves on these platforms.
- Then, the creditworthiness and risk appetite assessment is done by the platforms based on the amount and the needs of the borrower.

- Once the required documents are submitted online, the lending platform communicates the eligibility, terms and rates to the borrowers.
- Based on the eligibility, different product pages with payment terms and interest rates are offered to the borrower.
- Once the borrower selects the product package, the process is executed.
- This can typically take 24-72 hours.

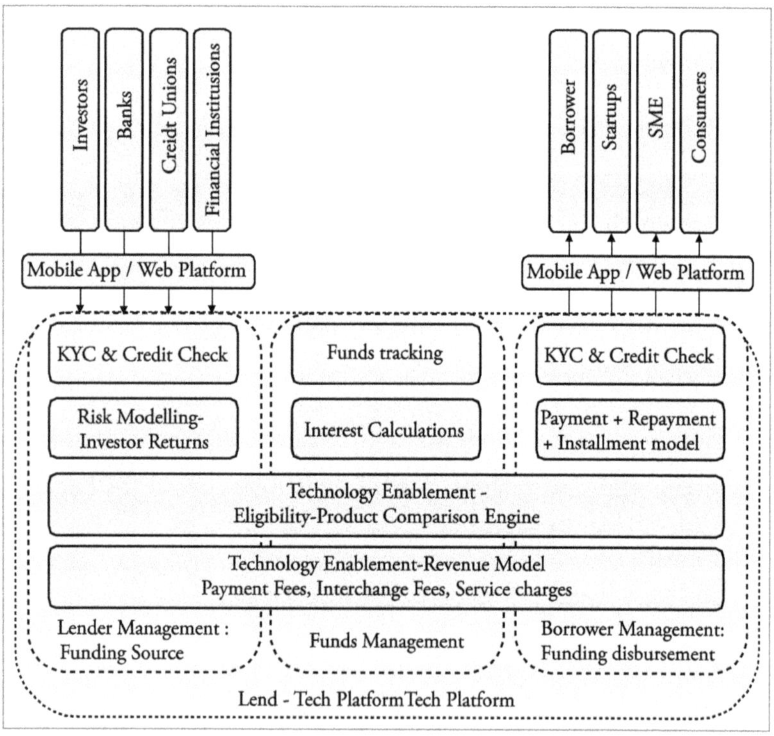

The Advantages of Lend-Tech Platforms

1. One-stop shop for all the borrowing needs
2. Connecting Lenders and borrowers together
3. Easy access for lenders to invest funds instead of trying to find the borrowers
4. Borrowers get a single platform to view and compare loan products based on their needs.
5. Avoids multiple visits to banks, filling lengthy forms and waiting for acceptance/rejection
6. Essentially Fintech Lending has made access to funds much easier for individuals and small businesses
7. Banks are not usually willing to lend to startups and small businesses due to a lack of financial history and high risk. This is where these platforms come into the picture. Lending companies have made significant efforts over the past 10-15 years to support this ecosystem resulting in the overall development of the economy and start-up as a whole.

Let us now look at some key aspects of Microfinancing.

8.3.2. Microfinance

Microfinance which includes Microlending and BNPL, are programs that help people who are at risk of being financially excluded. These groups of people include those without access to formal banking systems and people in remote and rural areas.

These programs provide small loans, usually between $50 and $1000, that allow people to start or expand small businesses, buy crops or livestock, or start an entrepreneurship program.

The term "microfinance" can apply to various activities. The microfinance industry refers to business lending for entrepreneurs in developing countries, which can include lending to consumers and to businesses.

Some microfinance organisations also provide services to small enterprises, such as business planning and coaching, while others offer financial services like savings and insurance. Microfinance can also refer to microfinance institutions, or MFIs, which are typically profit organisations. MFIs usually focus on serving the poor or low-income communities and often provide economic tools to uplift their participants.

Microfinance means different things to different people. In a nutshell, microfinance is the practice of helping impoverished communities expand their economic opportunities by helping them obtain loans for their businesses.

Generally, these microfinance loans allow people living in poverty to open small businesses or expand an existing one, such as a farm or taxi cab.

Here is how microfinance may affect you:

As an Investor/Lender,

Microfinance, or money lending to poor and low-income communities, is also known as microcredit, small loans, or microloans. It gives entrepreneurs the opportunity to start or expand small businesses and professionals the opportunity to start or expand a home-based business. This leads to economic development, providing jobs and income for otherwise impoverished communities. And as an investor, you think about whether the company you are investing in has exposure to microfinance, as those activities may have risk-return characteristics that may appeal to you.

- **As a Borrower,**

  Millions of people around the globe lack access to basic financial services, which often leads to a lack of food and medical care. Microfinance allows low-income individuals and communities to improve their quality of life through access to income, savings, and health services. Microfinance is not a handout; it is a tool. A tool that provides an opportunity for bettering people's lives and empowering them to improve their own situations.

- **Microlending**

  Microlending refers to small loans of money to minor businesses. These businesses are usually involved in small-scale agriculture, crafts, or commerce. When these small businesses have the money they need, they can grow and make more products, which creates more jobs. In this way, microlending helps the economy grow.

  The benefit of microlending to investors is permitting them a further portfolio of investment diversification. And they have great control over whom they lend the money to and how much they lend. As for the borrower, the benefit of microlending is the only way for them to secure their finances. Traditional financial institutions allow them even if they have bad credit or if they want to loan less than what is allowed.

- **BNPL: Buy Now Pay Later**

  Have you ever heard of a 'Buy Now Pay Later' offer? Or maybe you've heard about them but are not sure what they are? Well, BNPL (Buy Now Pay Later) is a short-term credit service that allows you to buy things you require now and pay in small instalments (usually weekly or fortnightly).

  It is mainly aimed at people who are in financial need and can't pay in full for an item such as a mobile phone, tablet, laptop, or other gadgets. These cards are issued by banks, credit unions, finance companies, and retailers. Some BNPL cards are only available in-store or at specific retailers and require regular payments to be cleared in full by the end of the promotional period.

  Others can be charged at any time but may have a high-interest rate. Buy now, pay later is fast becoming known in today's generation, with customers enjoying the BNPL offers.

8.3.3. Lend-Tech Companies

Let's take a look at some of the major players in the Lendtech arena globally, Klarna being the leader.

- **Klarna**

  Klarna is a Swedish Fintech company that provides payment services. Klarna's mission is to make paying for things as easy as possible, and that's exactly what it does. Klarna enables e-commerce by allowing consumers to pay in 30 days interest-free. (It's also possible to purchase now and pay later through Klarna, but that's beyond the scope of this brief intro.) Consumers can sign up for Klarna's services using their Visa or Mastercard and can utilise the Klarna Pay Later option when shopping on renowned e-commerce sites, including ASOS, Zara, and H&M.

Mission: Make paying as simple, safe and smooth as possible.

Vision: Transfer power from the large corporations to the consumer, and empower consumers to make fast and informed decisions.

Value Propositions:

- For Consumers: Simplified purchasing, more convenient buy now, pay later solution.
- For Merchants: Wider consumer reach via Klarna's platform and higher conversions via payment options

  There are other key players in this space providing technology platforms for lend-tech solutions.

- **PayPal**

  PayPal is an excellent payment service that many BNPL websites use to process payments. The PayPal service lets you send, receive, or request money, and you can easily send money between bank accounts, credit cards, and debit cards. PayPal accounts work with most major credit cards, and you can also use PayPal to buy things online or in stores.

- **AfterPay**

  AfterPay is one of the popular BNPL services. The AfterPay system allows you to make purchases in instalments rather than buying everything at once. There are three main ways AfterPay works. The standard option is for the merchant to deduct 25% of the item's purchase price from the customer's bank account in four equal payments spread across the month. The second option allows the merchant to deduct the full cost from the customer's bank account. The third option allows the merchant to collect the full amount from the customer's bank account at the first payment, along with 5% interest.

8.4. Insuretech - Applying Technology to the Insurance Industry

Insurtech is insurance technology, a Fintech sector used to refer to the technology adopted to augment and improve the operations of the insurance industry as a whole as well as for the consumers.

Technology companies - Bigtechs and startups alike are investing and assisting the insurance industry in building the required expertise to leverage technology. This includes AI/ML, RPA and Blockchain, which can be used from mobile devices, car infotainment systems, as well as consumer wearables. The insurance industry is being transformed by this, further enhancing the overall insurance issuance and claim processing multi-folds.

According to the 2019 World Insurance Report, traditional insurance companies and start-ups are discovering that collaboration offers a win-win way forward to optimise the use of technology. As per CB Insights, global investment in Insurtech rose from $348 million in 2012 to $4.15 billion in 2018.

This is not a surprise as this was the only way to be associated with the consumers in a connected digital era.

The democratisation of Fintech is greatly aided by the ease of the insurance process.

8.4.1. Insurance Business and Need for Insurtech

Historically, buying insurance is not a very straightforward process as one has to think of the negative events and estimate in terms of cost to mitigate these events.

1. The Insurance industry has often been shamed due to the sheer nature of the business and pushy sales agents. It is always ill-thought of as people widely believe that these agents are more focused on the commissions and do not always keep the customer's interests in mind.
2. The process also includes mammoth paperwork with a multitude of checks. In addition to this, there is large documentation in "small print" where there are different conditions and disclaimers for the claim process. This tiny print is full of confusing jargon, which is difficult for the common person to understand.
3. After spending weeks or even months reading through the extensive documentation, a claimant learns that the coverage is denied due to some provision or prerequisite.

4. This is the reason why people procrastinate buying insurance coverage or just refuse to purchase this very useful and vital financial instrument to cover the unthinkable.

With the availability of new technology, as mentioned in earlier sections, it is possible to augment and improve this tedious insurance buying and claiming process and reduce friction throughout the process.

Let us list the goals of Insurtech to understand this domain better:

- **a.** Setting up a comparison of several insurance packages with benefits and drawbacks, rendering insurance policies easier to understand.
- **b.** Facilitating ease of buying insurance, like buying a commodity on an e-commerce website.
- **c.** Offering insurance in a more implicit mechanism, e.g. if one is buying car insurance, it could be combined with a family cover.
- **d.** Optimizing effective paperwork like real-time KYCs and automated background checks.
- **e.** Additionally, regular collection of data using IoT devices like wearables or OBD devices (On Board Diagnostics) for automobiles. This data can be used during the claim process.
- **f.** Packaging together a range of options to offer easy-to-buy and claim insurance products.

8.4.2. The Insurtech Platform Model

Given below is a detailed pictorial representation of how an Insuretech platform functions. It is a high-level schematic of a typical Insuretech platform connecting the consumer with an insurance provider.

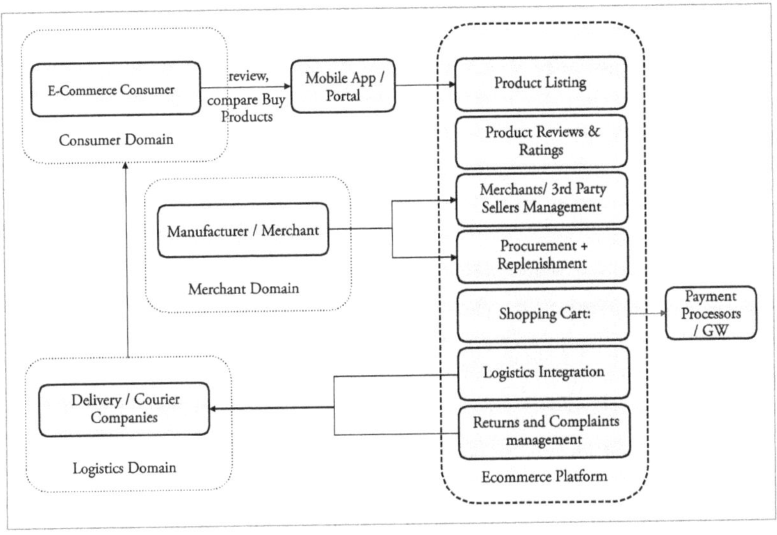

- The schematic shows the multiple steps involved, right from finding the right insurance product and buying it.
- The platform then executes the qualifying steps with the right background checks like - KYC and insurer details.
- There are additional checks in the insurtech connected ecosystem using IoT-Internet of Things, devices like Car OBD - onboard diagnostic.
- This provides the driving patterns, and car health, along with the other parameters.

- These parameters are inputs to the premium calculations on the Insuretech platform.
- The claims process is also simplified using these platforms with connected physical entities like car service centres for car insurance and hospitals for health insurance.

8.4.3. Insurtech Companies

Let us now take a look at some of the notable Insurtech companies globally-

1. **Lemonade:** Lemonade, founded in 2015 by Daniel Schreiber and Shai Winingeris a peer-to-peer insurance company that uses artificial intelligence and blockchain technology to simplify the insurance process. Lemonade has been praised for its innovative approach to insurance, and it has been named one of the most innovative companies in the world by Fast Company and Forbes. However, Lemonade has also been criticised for its high premiums and its lack of customer service.
2. **Oscar Health:** Oscar Health, founded in 2012 by Mario Schlosser, Josh Kushner, and Kevin Nazemi is a health insurance company that uses data and technology to provide more personalised and affordable health insurance plans. Oscar Health is pioneering into virtual care, In-Home care using the latest technologies like Artificial intelligence data analytics.
3. **Teladoc Health:** Teladoc Health, founded in 2002 by Jason Gorevic and Rudy Rubinstein, is a telehealth

company that specialises in video chat and phone consultations with doctors and other healthcare providers. Overall, Teladoc Health is a leading Insurtech company. The company uses a number of technologies to make healthcare more affordable, accessible, and user-friendly. Teladoc Health has over 50 million members in the United States and the United Kingdom, and it is headquartered in New York City.

8.5. WealthTech - Managing Wealth Using Technology

To explore this area, first, let us understand the concept of Wealth Management.

Wealth is measured in liquid cash as well as real estate possessions.

The management of wealth is to plan the growth of assets and mitigate any loss of value essentially by understanding the market dynamics and making adequate decisions to achieve financial goals.

Generally speaking, in a simple manner, wealth management is a process involving reviewing and tracking one's assets, corresponding to tax planning, and financial investments using available instruments to secure, grow and protect wealth.

The Four critical aspects of Wealth Management are:

- **Risk Assessment:** Adopting the right mix of aggressive and conservative measures to reach goals.

- **Investment Strategy:** The composition of investments from Government bonds to Cryptocurrencies.
- **Tax Advice:** Understanding different taxes and minimising the liability.
- **Asset Planning:** Leveraging assets to generate optimum returns.

8.5.1. Wealthtech Introduction

The wealth management sector of Fintech is in the middle of a drastic change. Classical methodologies and advice are becoming irrelevant. This has impacted everyone from the retail investor to the multi-million dollar individual and billion-dollar organisations managing their wealth portfolios.

These seismic changes must be attributed to the changing technology landscape across the overall Fintech industry.

According to recent statistics from the financial-technology analytical research firm FinTech Global, wealthtech is one of the top verticals of Fintech.

Overall funding for wealthtech has surged since 2015-2016, hitting almost $4.6 billion in 2018. The trend continues in 2020-2021.

This Wealthtech ecosystem is democratising a multitude of activities that were previously exclusive to experts and strives for efficiency in financial processes. It has promoted a drastic digital transformation and reformed the way modern finance could be applied to Wealth Management.

A combination of the words wealth and technology, the term wealthtech refers to those technology solutions that aim to augment and improve the wealth-management process.

As part of the Fintech domain, wealthtech is specifically concerned with digital transformation using technology that can improve wealth management and investing, especially with respect to ease of processing, affordability and accessibility to multiple services from a single platform.

This has become an increasingly challenging market because of the greater regulatory and compliance responsibilities, startups hotting up the ecosystem by competing and, at times collaborating with the traditional portfolio management houses.

The Wealthtech industry is extensively investing in technology to build solutions using AI/ML, biometrics, and Natural Language processing. At the same time, making this technology easily accessible for investors over smartphones.

One of the most widely used Wealtech instruments is RoboAdvisory.

This technology-based automated service involves determining the investment instruments depending on the risk preferences, fee optimization and value generation using machine learning. Implying that the complete replacement of human input by RoboAdvisory is something that the industry is striving for, as the parameters are pretty dynamic. This is due to the sheer nature of the connected world that is impacted by geopolitical situations, trade wars and global supply chains.

8.5.2. The Wealthtech Platform Model

The high-level schematic of a typical Wealthtech platform connecting the investor and the wealth instruments below gives you complete detail on the functioning of the wealthtech platform.

Wealthtech is one of the fastest growing Fintech domains.

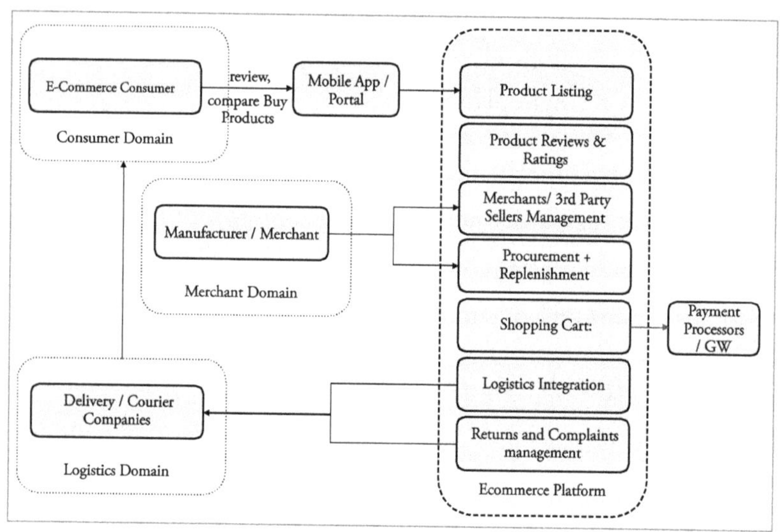

The schematic shows the feature stack for processing investments on behalf of the investor by a wealthtech platform.

Let us now look at the various components, tools & disruptions in the Wealthtech space.

- **Marketplaces**

  Wealthtech marketplaces are third-party investment models that retain control of allocation, trade implementation, and rebalancing. Marketplace models in wealth management are emerging as hybrid business models that offer a combination of digital and human engagement, supporting wealthtech platforms to focus more on client-building and retention strategies while offering lower costs and maintaining discretion.

- **Trading Instruments**

  Trading instruments are general wealth management tools suitable for users of any expertise level. They allow users to trade in multiple financial asset types, offer advanced financial chart comparison tools, provide research-backed analysis on financial markets and investments from top analysts, and are available on multiple devices.

- **Wealth Portfolio**

  A Wealth Portfolio helps investors and financial advisors unify and manage their investment portfolios in a single view. The service offers innovative multi-asset class portfolio analysis for wealth managers and individuals to manage the risk and performance parameters of their investments.

- **Compliance Management & Tax Planning**

  Compliance & wealthtech with the help of technological solutions, goes hand in hand with regulatory processes & tax management within the financial industry.

- **RoboAdvisors**

  These are automated services using Artificial Intelligence, leveraging Machine Learning algorithms to offer financial advice or investment management online, with little to no human interaction. This service can offer customers ideal investment portfolios based on their risk preferences and the most profitable investment options in the market. Robo-advisors today replace or complement traditional financial advisors, as they can generate revenues through lower margins and higher volumes of transactions.

- **Quant advisors**

  Another extension of robo-advisors consists of quant advisors. These systems deal with quantitative investing — the use of quantitative strategies to create mathematical models that ingest quantitative data from market feeds and other sources. The data is analysed with the help of a computational model designed to exploit inefficiencies. When the code spots a positive trend or locates an inefficiency, it triggers the appropriate buys and sells.

- **Algorithmic Trading**

  This form of trading uses complex formulas and mathematical models combined with human oversight to make decisions to buy or sell financial securities on an exchange. Algorithmic trading can be used in a wide variety of situations — for example, order execution, arbitrage, or trend trading strategies.

8.6. ECOM Revolution

E-commerce, or electronic commerce, is a modern age Fintech industry sector that is democratising the marketplace for merchants and consumers alike. A handy tool for manufacturers & retailers to increase sales through internet-based online commerce and multiply revenue by reaching consumers which they would not otherwise. During the COVID Pandemic 2020-2021, this was the most utilised mode of processing purchases worldwide.

According to statistics, global e-commerce sales could reach $6.542 trillion by 2023, representing 22% of the total retail market. With access to the internet and global marketplace in today's day and age, a large section of consumers are logging on to these portals for online shopping. As mentioned earlier, e-commerce has surpassed sales in physical stores multifold during the pandemic. As life is returning to normal, businesses are being opened, and e-commerce sales are growing. This is something that has changed in the last decade from consumers' ease of view.

8.6.1. Advantages of e-commerce for Consumers

1. **Lower prices:** The lower costs of running an e-commerce store versus a physical store translates to cost savings for the consumer. This is one of the biggest e-commerce advantages. Online prices are typically lower than traditional store prices, and e-commerce sites are able to offer more discounts and promotions that are easier to claim.
2. **Convenient and safe:** Shopping when you want, from where you want, is far preferable (and a whole lot safer) than heading out in this COVID reality we're now living in. Coronavirus aside, there's also something to be said about shopping from your bedroom without having to venture out, wait in lines, battle the cold weather, and all other challenges that go with consumerism.
3. **Wide product variety:** In the global marketplace that is the internet, consumers can buy electronics from China, books from England, clothes from Paris, and good old US products all from the comfort of their homes. The width and depth of products sold online are unbeatable.

4. **More informed decision-making:** Information is literally at your fingertips when buying online, including:

   i. Reviews from real customers

   ii. Product descriptions

   iii. Usage videos

   iv. Product guides

   v. Social validation

   Comparison shopping is another top benefit of e-commerce for consumers, who can easily compare products, brands, and websites, with even side-by-side comparison possible. Many comparison shopping sites exist with the sole purpose of enabling consumers to compare products side-by-side based on price and discount metrics.

5. **Saves time:** In an age where time is a rare commodity, shopping online provides massive time savings for the consumer. Since 63% of consumers start their shopping journey online, it makes sense to be able to buy where you already are (Thinkwithgoogle, 2018). No need to head out, shop in-store, wait in line, and then journey back home when you can access a greater product variety at a lower price from the comfort of home.

8.6.2. Advantages of e-commerce to Businesses

1. **Lower costs:** Going online eradicates the need for a physical storefront, meaning lower fixed costs for the business. Also, since most e-commerce is automated, fewer staff members are required. Marketing an e-commerce

store using Google Adwords, e-commerce Facebook advertising, and social media marketing, for example, are much more cost-effective than promoting offline. These cost savings translate to lower prices for the consumer and more sales for the business. This is one of the key benefits of e-commerce for businesses.

2. **Customer data:** S selling online gives the retailer access to a customer data goldmine that is just not accessible through brick-and-mortar retailing. Not only do online consumers typically provide their name, email address, and phone number when checking out or registering on a site, but a wealth of consumer behaviour and demographic data, available through Google Analytics. This can help online retailers optimise the consumer journey and market more effectively and accurately. E-tailers are also able to nurture and retarget consumers precisely, based on their stage in the journey. For example, using data insights, an online retailer can email potential customers who have abandoned their carts, motivating and reminding them to check out their purchase, and can even use retargeting advertising to nurture leads that are not yet purchased.

3. **Wider customer base:** Going online with e-commerce sites makes geographical boundaries inconsequential. You could sell your products to online shoppers across the country or even across the globe. You're not limited to shoppers in your physical location.

   The internet also opens up your retail store to different niche audiences that you wouldn't have access to. By using multiple online touchpoints, you can access customers from all angles by going where they already are, such as social media, forums, and Google searches.

4. **Open always:** When you sell online, your business is open 24/7/365. Even though your customer support may be sleeping, automation ensures that the rest of the sales process is always flowing and consumers can buy on any day, at any time.
5. **Easier to scale up:** Scaling up or growing a physical store requires more floor space (and the expense that comes with it!), employees, and shelf space. In contrast, it's very simple to grow an online store, which is one of the less obvious benefits of e-commerce for businesses.

All you need is more inventory, a few digital tweaks, and possibly more storage space, which is far less costly than storefront space. Being online also eliminates the need for opening a new store in another location, as you're already within the reach of a global marketplace.

8.6.3. ECommerce Types

The simplest e-commerce definition is "commercial transactions conducted over the internet" or internet commerce.

Basically, it's nothing more than buying something online or online shopping. If you're one of the millions of people who shop on Amazon, you're already familiar with e-commerce from the consumer's point of view.

This is how e-commerce typically works-

- It's a two-party transaction – usually either business-to-business (B2B) or business-to-consumer (B2C).
- The seller lists products or services for sale online through an online B2B platform of their choice.
- The customer (either another business or a direct consumer) finds the product and buys it online.
- Digital products are delivered to the buyer right away. Physical products are shipped to the buyer's chosen address.

Though not as common as B2B and B2C, there are a couple of other e-commerce business models:

- **Consumer-to-Consumer** (C2C): With this approach, consumers sell directly to one another. This is made possible with e-commerce platforms like eBay, LetGo, Poshmark, and Mercari. Some platforms let customers create online stores which they can use to sell items they already own or to sell items they find elsewhere.
- **Consumer-to-Business** (**C2B**): With this method, a consumer is selling something to a business. For instance, some artists sell their work for display in other businesses. It's also C2B when photographers sell photos to stock photo companies for use online.

8.6.4. The e-Commerce Model Platform

A high-level schematic of a typical e-commerce platform connecting consumers & businesses is shown below. It gives you complete detail on the functioning of the platform.

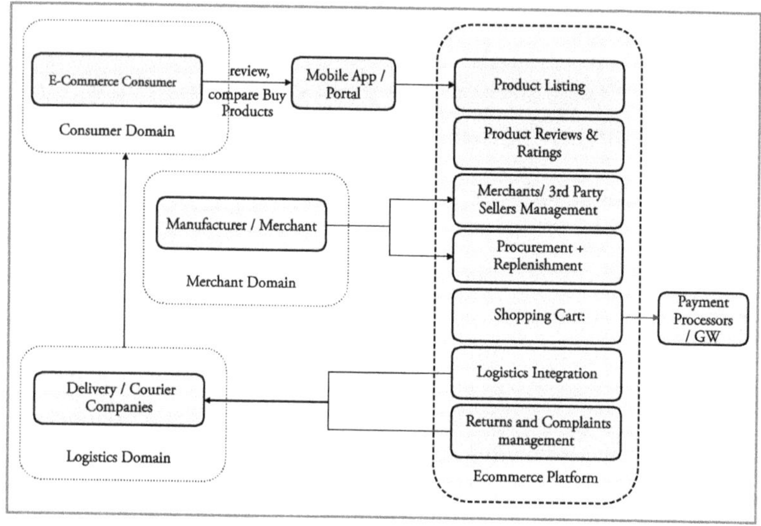

An e-commerce website is a place where content and technology come together to enable purchases. It is important for the e-commerce platform to do the following in addition to the standard e-commerce platform components to attract a larger consumer base.

These include:

- Ecommerce search engine optimization (SEO)
- Content marketing
- Influencer marketing
- Email marketing
- Online advertising

- Listing products on online marketplaces
- Using social media platforms to connect with target audiences
- Other e-commerce marketing methods

8.7. PayTech or PaymentTech

Payment technology is at the core of the Fintech ecosystem. Paytech connects the consumer with the services provider for payment of products and services. Omni-channel payment is a combination of retail payment and e-commerce payment.

Retail payment in-store where the consumer avails the products and services in person. E-Commerce is payment over the webpage for the product and services.

8.7.1. QR Code Payments

The fastest growing QR code payment system is the Indian NPCI-National Payments Corporation of India based Bharat QR.

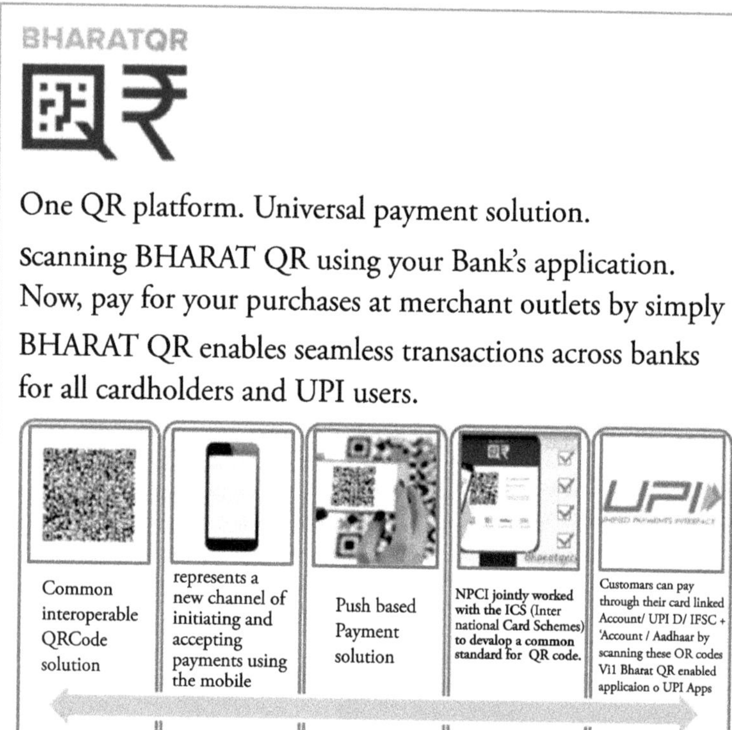

Ref: NPCI

The TEN Steps of the QR code Payment System consists of the following parties-

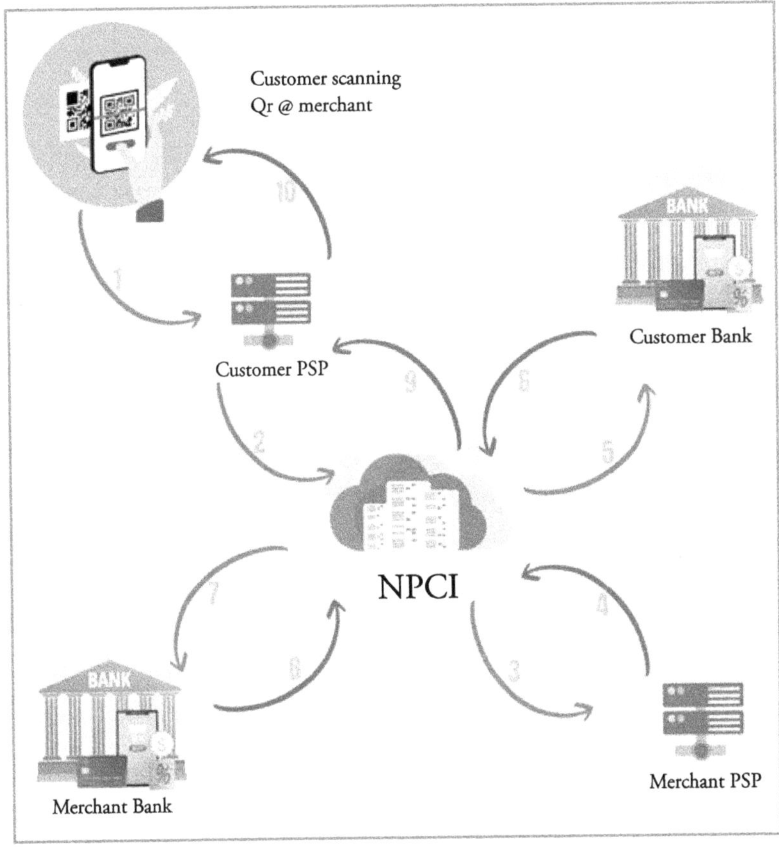

- The Acquirer – merchant on boarding, merchant management, and merchant mobile app solutions
- The Issuer – consumer on-boarding and consumer mobile app solutions
- The Transaction Processing Engine (NPCI) - end transaction routing engine

- The Customer PSP - Payment Service Provider whose mobile application customer is using
- The Merchant PSP - Payment Service Provider, where Merchant account is linked for processing the transactions

Individuals and businesses increasingly adopt Fintech, like digital financial management tools, banking solutions, wallets, and payments, which promote faster transactions, better financial wellness, and greater access to capital.

Fintech software solutions and infrastructure significantly optimise how financial service providers operate and support broader industry growth. Today, banking solutions and digital payment alongside personal finance tools are revolutionising how people transact and manage their finances. While solutions designed for financial sectors significantly enhance how financial institutions operate.

The impact of Fintech extends beyond the financial system as it serves as a catalyst and core component of digitalization. Retail investing, consumer finance, the gig economy, e-commerce, and other innovations attribute the recent and rapid growth to Fintech enablers that power digital transformation.

8.7.2. Financial Inclusion

New initiatives are available to enable financial inclusions, such as

- **QR Codes**

  QR codes are a promising way to get more customers to go digital and digitalize payments at low-income merchants.

This is because QR codes:

- Make it easier to increase the acceptance networks' size
- Provide an elegant and effective solution to the card distribution challenge
- Provide a more convenient user experience

- **BNPL**

  Buy Now, Pay Later (BNLP) provides the consumer with an improved checkout experience. Also, it offers an interest-free alternative to credit cards. It promises to provide sustainable and accessible credit to underbanked and unbanked consumers.

- **Biometric Authentication**

  Fintech companies are provided with biometrically verified customer identities to support financial inclusion. Startups use mobile phone cameras to obtain fingerprints and national database verification.

- **Agriculture-Linked Financing**

  A digital financial and agricultural model is available for agricultural investors and farmers. Potential investors can use a platform to find the most relevant and suitable farms to invest in.

- **Rural Digital Financial Management**

  Fintech largely depends on the participation of people, which drives companies to simplify basic financial operations for rural and remote regions. This initiative empowers communities to remotely monitor and manage their transactions and monetary savings.

- **Livestock-Backed Financial Services**

  Many blockchain-based financial platforms are now accepting livestock as collateral. The livestock-as-an-asset model enables smaller farmers to maximise the livestock-rearing benefits. The platforms also improve access to banking products for SMEs and women.

8.7.3. EdTech - a Fintech Applicative Industry Story

Educational technology (EdTech) supports online learning among schools, colleges, and universities and proved especially useful during the pandemic. For this segment, there is a strong Fintech platform that supports add-on payments, recurring payments, pay-as-you-go payments, etc.

The emerging EdTech tools and products enable schools to raise standards, save time, and increase engagement between students, parents/guardians, and teachers. This creates a positive impact across the education spectrum.

The platform handles all aspects of payments cost-effectively, quickly, easily, and electronically. Schools do not need to deal with the pain of reconciling and handling cash from parents/guardians. Instead, they gain full control over the payments from tutors, clubs, trips, and meals instantly, seamlessly, and effortlessly.

With the quick integration through unified API and built-in compliance, payments between schools and parents become instant, easy, and secure.

Summary

- The 5G evolution in revolutionising Fintech connections. It is a major technological leap making the task of financial transactions even more seamless, especially in rural areas
- Fintech is also supporting a new business model of the `Sharing economy'. The art of allowing people to share underutilised resources is the `Sharing economy'. Popular examples are Airbnb and Uber.
- All these are connected and interrelated and owe their prevalence to the rise of mobile technology, the internet and the demand for convenience and flexibility.
- Various types of platforms summarised below are offering many benefits to consumers in their day-to-day life.
- As the name suggests, Lend Tech is a Fintech domain that provides loans and other forms of financial services to consumers. Bringing borrowers and lenders together on the same platform makes transactions so smooth. However, there are certain risks involved, like high-interest rates and fraudulent practices.
- Similarly, there is Insurtech which uses technology in the insurance sector—to assist people in comparing insurance policies, buying the best suitable policy online and claiming insurance.
- Applying technology to wealth management is Wealthtech. Particularly using AI/ML, Biometrics, and natural language processing to extend personalised and automated services.

- Paytech for payments and Edutech, denoting educational technology, are other similar systems. Key benefits accruing from all these are transparency, easy accessibility, and value for money.
- Besides this, another area that is democratising the business environment today is `E-commerce'. The advantages e-commerce extends for retailers and consumers are immense. Four main types are B2B, B2C, C2C, and C2B.

Currency adapts to human evolution, from bronze to printed money and now transitioning to digital currency.

Chapter 9

Decentralise Finance

Democratisation enables consumers to use financial services across industries. We have gone through multiple aspects of financial technologies, how the new platforms are augmenting and enhancing the existing financial services, as well as providing new avenues in the financial services sector.

This current trend of Democratising the services for easy access to everyone is adopted all across the world in multiple Fintech Sectors.

Let us move to the next step of the Decentralisation of Fintech.

9.1. Platform limitations of existing systems

We have reviewed multiple democratisation models in earlier sections. One critical component of this model is the Platform that is used to provide financial services. This platform is at the core of the model and orchestrates Fintech solutions with the help of internal and external systems.

First, I'd like you to refer to the high-level depiction of the traditional centralised approach below.

There are intrinsic limitations to this approach.

1. The platform orchestrates the Fintech solution flow
2. The decision-making business logic resides within the configuration of the platform
3. These platforms are managed & controlled by big corporations

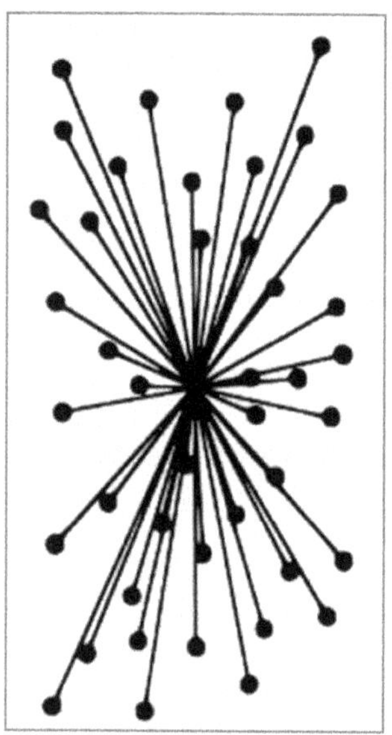

4. Small and medium-sized enterprises have to comply with these platforms and work according to the intersection points defined by the platform
5. The data storage and usage are generally managed by the corporation based on their interpretation of the regional data protection regulatory frameworks. Still this is a grey area "Who owns the data?". The data can be used for multiple uses and even questionable intentions at times.

6. The fees and charging models are defined by the corporation owning the platform, and based on their internal and external parameters, these are subject to change.
7. In essence, these modern multinational corporations are replacing traditional banks as the engines driving Fintech solutions along with the banks in the majority of the cases
8. Generally, these corporations are big tech companies acquiring smaller Fintech solution players or Conglomerates of multinational banks creating entities for specific Fintech solutions
9. So Democratisation does take place in terms of service usage, but the service is owned by big corporations
10. In case of scenarios where there is a security breach or malpractice, these companies get highly impacted, causing an outage of the services, which affects hundreds of thousands if not millions of Fintech services users
11. At the same time, scaling of these services entirely depends on the investment, operational and support appetite of the corporations, which may limit certain services to certain regions.
12. Also, there are intermediaries to simplify access to the platform. In many cases, the intermediaries extend the services to consumers instead of consumers having direct connection to the platform.

9.2. Need for Decentralised Finance (DeFi)

Over the last couple of years, "DeFi" has picked quite a name for itself, especially in the global tech community.

Many in the community believe that DeFi, or decentralised finance, can completely turn the global economy on its head by making the finance sector transparent and more easily accessible.

The DeFi movement is the migration of technology from Platform to Network Journey.

Please refer to the schematic topology of the approach change from a "centralised platform, an Inside-out strategy" to a "De-Centralised Network and an outside-in strategy" detailed in the diagram below.

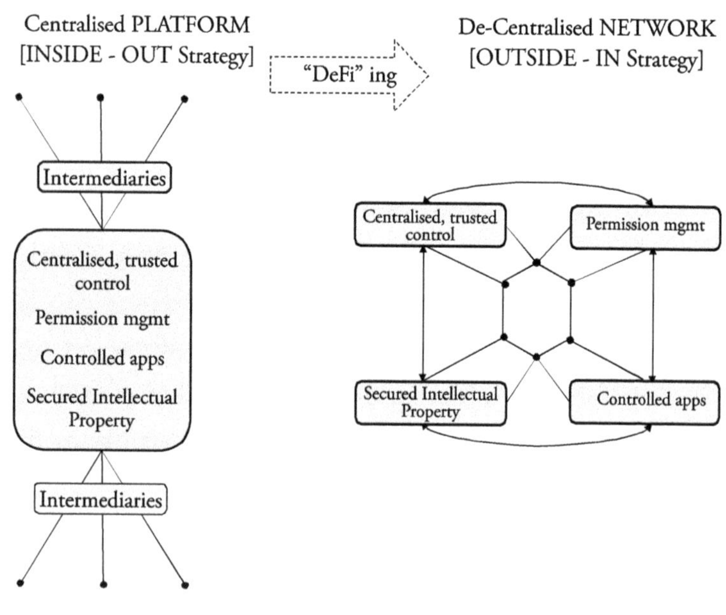

9.2.1. Aspects of DeFi

Let us now explore in detail the critical aspects of Decentralised Finance one by one.

1. **Decentralisation:** Multiple copies of the required data elements across the network, augmented with specific attributes. This negates the need for centralised controlling authority. And also greatly reduces dependency on a specific finance system that is dependent on the whims of a central regulator. That's one of the most exciting promises of DeFi.
2. **Transparency:** Since everyone in the network maintains a copy of relevant data, all the data stored inside is accessible based on the network-identified permission.
3. **Permissionless:** A public network can be utilised by consumers and enterprises in the same way. It creates an open system where people from around the world– who don't have access to sophisticated financial services– can participate without going through extensive red tape.
4. **Trustless:** In a decentralised system, individual network nodes have an economic incentive to work in the interest of the system in addition to tangible and intangible benefits from the network. This is in absolute contrast to the traditional financial system, where you need to trust a centralised governing body to do its job well.
5. **Censorship Resistance:** By definition, these copies are tamper-proof, and only entities who are entitled by the network can access them. Hence the data is immutable

at the same time, augmentable, enhancing the whole tracking and monitoring of the system.

6. **Programmable:** These decentralised networks have a basic genome of open-source systems, and they welcome developers from all around the world to create their own unique applications on top of them. This openness to innovation has led to the creation of some fantastic DeFi applications - DApps.
7. **DAPP:** The applications which work on decentralised platforms, the data that they require/produce need not be processed by a central server/entity, are called decentralised applications. They don't require a middleman to function or manage a user's information.

9.2.2. Advantages of DeFi over Traditional Finance

	Traditional Finance	DeFi
Trust Allocation	System and policies controlled by Corporations, bankers and regulators.	An inbuilt incentivization system negates the need to trust a Third-party. Network, by definition built on incentivised trust.
Transparency	Extremely opaque since bigTechs and banks are unwilling to expose their internal operations to the public for confidentiality purposes.	The DeFi ecosystem has a permissionless and transparent system.
Innovations	System burdened by cumbersome red tape that inhibits innovation.	An open-source protocol that encourages developers to build and create their own applications.

In the subsequent sections of Defi, we dive into the details of the key components and new technology enabling Decentralised finance.

9.3. Blockchain For Finance

Blockchain and DeFi always come together. Blockchain is the key ingredient of the Decentralised finance industry. The underlying Blockchain networks enable DeFi networks.

From the inception of Bitcoin, the blockchain innovation was intended to move assets from point A to point B without a focal governing body.

As blockchains have advanced, they've had the option to accomplish a lot quicker with cheaper exchanges. One of the highly used networks is RippleNet. This is based on Ripple, an organisation that utilises blockchain innovation for RippleNet, a worldwide payment network. RippleNet exchanges process in a span of seconds and cost a negligible part of a penny.

Monetary foundations that utilise blockchain innovation definitely offer a more proficient approach to Fintech. Those worldwide financial transactions that would normally take hours are now possible in seconds using these networks.

Added transaction security: Financial organisations are generally focused on computerised transactions, specifically to convey the metadata accumulated during the transaction cycle when they go through transaction payment settlement processors and banks. In stark contrast, Blockchains utilise cryptographic calculations to process and record exchange blocks. This cryptography could be a way for transaction processing entities to reduce the overhead of exchanging additional data during transaction processing.

Smart Contracts

Ethereum (CRYPTO: ETH) in 2015 was a significant step in the right direction for blockchain innovation. It was the first blockchain to have Smart Contracts.

A smart contract is a self-executing contract with the terms of the agreement between buyer and seller being directly written into lines of code. The code and the agreements contained therein exist across a distributed, decentralised blockchain network. The code controls the execution, and transactions are trackable and irreversible.

Smart contracts permit trusted transactions and agreements to be carried out among disparate, anonymous parties without the need for a central authority, legal system, or external enforcement mechanism. This makes smart contracts substantially more efficient.

Nick Szabo, an American computer scientist who invented a virtual currency called "Bit Gold" in 1998, defined smart contracts as computerised transaction protocols that execute the terms of a contract.

Smart contracts deployed to blockchains render transactions traceable, transparent, and irreversible.

9.3.1. Smart Contract Usages

Smart Contracts can be used in a variety of use cases, especially in the DeFi ecosystem.

1. **KYC:** Know Your Customer: Smart contracts provide a secure environment making the KYC less susceptible to tampering and easy to access. The KYC Smart Contract stores the hash of the KYC details on the financial network. This Smart Contract is layered on top of the actual financial transaction so that whenever a transaction is to be initiated, a KYC Smart contract is executed to secure the transaction on DeFi Network.
2. **Financial services:** Smart contracts help in transforming traditional financial services in multiple ways. In the case of insurance claims, they perform error checking, routing, and transfer payments to the user if everything is found appropriate.

Smart contracts incorporate critical tools for bookkeeping and eliminate the possibility of infiltration of accounting records. They also enable shareholders to take part in decision-making in a transparent way. Also, they help in trade clearing, where the funds are transferred once the amounts of trade settlements are calculated.

9.3.2. Smart Contract Benefits and Limitations

What are Smart Contracts Benefits?

1. **Autonomy and savings:** Smart contracts avoid other intermediaries to confirm the agreement; thus, they eliminate the risk of overcorrection or manipulation by third parties. Moreover, the absence of intermediaries in smart contracts results in substantial cost savings.
2. **Backup:** All the documents stored on the blockchain are duplicated multiple times; Because of this, originals can be restored in the event of any data loss.
3. **Safety:** Smart contracts are encrypted, and cryptography keeps all the documents safe from alterations.
4. **Speed:** Smart contracts automate tasks by using computer protocols, saving hours of lengthy business processes.
5. **Accuracy:** Using smart contracts results in the elimination of errors that occur due to manual filling of numerous forms.

The major limitations of Smart Contracts:

1. **Difficult to change:** Changing smart contract processes is almost impossible. Any error in the code can be time-consuming and expensive to correct, as this is a part of the wider network and already spread to numerous nodes across the network.
2. **Possibility of loopholes:** According to the concept of good faith, parties will deal fairly and not get benefits unethically from a contract. However, using smart contracts renders it hard to ensure that the terms are met according to what was agreed upon.

3. **Third party:** Although smart contracts seek to eliminate third-party involvement, it is not possible to eliminate them. Third parties assume different roles from the ones they take in traditional contracts. For example, lawyers will not be needed to prepare individual contracts; however, they will be needed by developers to understand the terms to create codes for smart contracts. So the development of Smart Contracts need specialised financial and Legal know-how from experts.
4. **Vague terms:** Since contracts include terms that are not always understood, smart contracts are not always able to handle terms and conditions that are vague.

Visa (NYSE: V) is one of the biggest instalment processors on the planet, and it was perhaps the earliest major monetary organisation to embrace blockchain innovation. Given below is the way Visa has utilised and created it:

In 2015, Visa was essential for a $30 million interest in Chain. com, a blockchain engineer.

In 2017, it sent off Visa B2B Connect, which utilises blockchain for global business-to-business instalments.

It has worked with digital currency trades and stages to send off cryptographic money charges and Visas.

Visa turned into the primary significant instalments organisation to settle exchanges with digital currencies in March 2021.

Barclays PLC (NYSE: BCS) is a global bank that has done an extensive study of blockchain innovation in finance. It has experimented with the utilisation of savvy agreements to exchange subsidiaries like prospects and choices. In the event that stock trades start involving shrewd agreements for subordinates, it could eliminate the time it takes to set up these agreements. The bank likewise recorded a patent application in 2018 to utilise blockchain in smoothing out the KYC cycle.

Alongside other large banks, Barclays is a financial backer, a venture to make computerised money variants of the U.S. dollar and a few other significant monetary forms. It will probably use blockchain innovation for quicker and less expensive exchanges.

American Express (NYSE: AXP) is both an instalment organisation and a monetary establishment offering credit and charged cards, banking, and credits. Lately, it has dealt with coordinating blockchain into its famous Membership Rewards program.

Working with the organisation Hyperledger, American Express fabricated its own in-house blockchain that it tried with Boxed, a web-based staple conveyance stage. This innovation permitted the shipper to offer more focus in view of various factors, such as the item bought or the hour of the day. At the point when a client made a buy that satisfied the circumstances, American Express acknowledged them for focus and charged the dealer through a brilliant agreement.

Shifting to blockchain innovation is costly and tedious, particularly since talented blockchain designers are hard to find. Some monetary organisations, especially the modest ones, might be hesitant to focus on upgrading existing frameworks.

Blockchain information can't be adjusted. Albeit, this is an advantage of utilising blockchain. It likewise has disadvantages for monetary organisations that frequently need to update information. To carry out blockchain, these organisations would have to change their philosophy.

Since blockchain innovation is moderately new and growing so rapidly, controllers haven't paced themselves up yet. Legislatures will doubtlessly establish arrangements that influence blockchain and the organisations utilising it.

The future of blockchain in finance

Right now, we're still in the beginning phases of both blockchain's turn of events and its utilisation in the monetary administration industry. Two of the greatest blockchain advancements to pay special attention to are upgrades in exchange handling and interoperability; these ought to make it highly beneficial for monetary organisations.

Prior blockchains were restricted as far as exchange handling is concerned. Bitcoin can deal with around three to five exchanges each second, and Ethereum can presently just handle around 10 to 15. That is not anywhere close enough to rival significant instalment processors like Visa, which can deal with around 1,700 exchanges each second.

Later blockchains have focused on versatility with quicker exchanges. The most outstanding digital money project in such a manner is Solana (CRYPTO: SOL), which flaunts top exchange seasons of 65,000 every second.

Another change we're seeing is a shift toward interoperability. Most blockchains to this point have been independent undertakings. In any case, different activities have arisen determined to work with correspondence between those different blockchains.

Blockchains will not totally supplant existing monetary frameworks at any point in the near future. Considering everything, monetary organisations are anticipated to utilise blockchain in trials to determine its capacity. Afterwards, step by step, coordinate it as an enhancement to their current frameworks.

Carrying out blockchain innovation is accompanied by challenges. In spite of the difficulties, many monetary organisations have begun utilising it, and blockchain stocks have become well-known ventures to open doors. Obviously, businesses comprehend the expected benefits that blockchain will be a developing piece of finance.

9.4. Applying Blockchain to Decentralise Finance

Bitcoin is the most well-known cryptocurrency, but it's not the only type of cryptocurrency out there. A "cryptocurrency" is simply a form of digital money that uses encryption to secure transactions and provides decentralised control. Because cryptocurrency is decentralised, it's created and controlled by a community of users rather than by an institution or government. Some cryptocurrencies can be mined, while others are traded on peer-to-peer exchanges.

- **What is Decentralised Finance?**

  Decentralised Finance is a concept used by cryptocurrencies that promise unconventional distributed control and less risk for investors. Traditional crypto funding involves the exchange of fiat currency for cryptocurrency. Investors put their money to work, buying crypto based on future projections of its value. Suppose the value of the crypto goes up; investors profit. If the value of the crypto goes down, investors lose.

  DeFi has seen tremendous growth in the past few years, especially in the last 12 months. The scope of DeFi is extensive.

  Currently, there are four main categories of DeFi:

  - Crypto Loans
  - Decentralised Exchanges
  - Stablecoins
  - Decentralised Asset Management.

- **What is the use of Decentralised Finance?**

  Decentralised Finance is a growing movement and a potential game-changer for the global finance industry. The term decentralised Finance refers to financial applications that work without a centralised controlling authority like a regional/national central bank. The applications these decentralised finance solutions provide significantly allow individuals and financial institutions to operate with minimal fees and, in most cases, zero fees.

  Decentralised Finance, or DeFi, is a nascent technology that aims to revolutionise how money works. Instead of relying on a bank or other traditional financial institution to hold users' funds, DeFi uses a decentralised network that relies on blockchain technology. The network allows users to store, send, and receive money without having to go through a formal financial institution first.

DeFi benefits include:

- **Financial Freedom:** Decentralised Finance is rapidly growing in adoption and popularity with the rise of cryptocurrencies and blockchain. Decentralisation creates a more level playing field for all participants. It not only places more power in people's hands but removes the need for middlemen. Decentralised Finance also serves as an excellent solution for global financial inclusion. By enabling more people to invest in assets and businesses, more individuals can have access to and reap the benefits of financial freedom.
- **Lower Transaction Fees:** Like any other technological breakthrough, Blockchain technology is constantly evolving and adding value to the lives of users everywhere. Decentralizing Finance using blockchain technology allows new startups and organisations to join the decentralised finance ecosystem without the need first to have the capital and technical knowledge to set up a full-fledged enterprise. One of the biggest benefits of decentralised Finance is the lower transaction fee. You may not realise this, but every exchange charges you transaction fees. For instance, Coinbase has a 2.9% fee if you send Bitcoin, Ethereum, or

Litecoin. But you don't have to pay this fee on decentralised exchanges like EtherDelta, Bisq, and ForkDelta. These exchanges operate on smart contract technology, which means there is no middleman like Coinbase. These exchanges aren't regulated, and they don't require personal information. They also don't store your money in a centralised location, which protects you against hackers.

- **Increased Security:** Cryptocurrency transactions are either irreversible, like Bitcoin transactions. Some, like Bitcoin, have strong fraud protection. Others, like Monero, have none. Decentralised Finance (DeFi) is reducing the risks associated with irreversible currency networks by improving existing financial technology (Fintech).

  It's improving on Bitcoin, Ethereum, and Ripple by adding trustless transactions, advanced consensus algorithms, and decentralised marketplaces. The Decentralised Finance (DeFi) space continues to grow and has many great benefits to users, such as increased security. DeFi is a decentralised platform that uses blockchain technology to store digital assets like cryptocurrencies and tokens. The platform allows users to create and use smart contracts, which are computer programs that automatically execute when certain conditions are met. The benefits of DeFi include increased security.

- **Low Barriers to Entry:** Blockchain technology is increasingly finding its place in the financial services industry. While Bitcoin was the first and best-known application of blockchain technology, the technology is being explored for its use in many more areas, including Finance. Currently, many financial companies are working on enhancing legacy systems to better utilise blockchain. The decentralised nature of blockchain also means that there is no single entity that controls a blockchain network. This eliminates the entry barriers that banks and other traditional financial companies face.

- **What are the Potential downsides of Decentralised Finance?**

  Decentralisation is a word that gets thrown around a lot these days. But what does it mean, really? Free yourself from centralised control. That's what it means. Decentralisation is a method of achieving economic freedom. It democratises economic and political power, allowing people to own and govern themselves.

  Decentralisation also challenges the centralised control structures that tend to strangle individuals, businesses, and countries. Decentralised Finance (DeFi) is a fast-growing subset of cryptocurrency investing, giving investors more choice in how to invest.

  DeFi uses smart contracts on blockchain to allow people to borrow money, lend money, and operate their own financial trading platforms, all without going through a third party.

Decentralisation, the philosophy that power is transferred from a central entity to an individual or a group, is gaining momentum in Finance. Bitcoin and other decentralised forms of currency have a growing group of supporters who believe this decentralised form of Finance will change the world. While decentralised Finance may indeed be the future of money, many experts say blockchain—the technology behind Bitcoin and other decentralised digital currencies—is yet to live up to its promises.

In 2023 and beyond, DeFi, Fintech, and Insurtech will continue uniting considerably.

Accordingly, people and organisations are searching for new and inventive ways of protecting and becoming rich.

- **Enter DeFi**

  One such inventive & strong option is decentralised money, or DeFi - an umbrella term for monetary administrations fueled by the blockchain framework. With DeFi, shoppers can do a vast majority of things that banks support - procure revenue, get loans, purchase protection, exchange subordinates, exchange resources, and that's only the tip of the iceberg. - Nevertheless, in a smoother way as it doesn't need desk work or an outsider.

  DeFi has been getting forward momentum, powered by the way that it diminishes human blunders through brilliant agreements, gives admittance to business sectors from any place, whenever, with a web association, and removes delegates.

Generally, DeFi transforms cash into a programmable and interoperable convention, similar to prior forms of the web digitised data and content.

While DeFi is a moderately late pattern, the amount secured in DeFi conventions has grown to more than $200 billion, with exchanging volumes coming to nearly $100 billion every month. The DeFi environment itself is quickly extending as far as broadening from Ethereum to different blockchain foundations (for example, Close, Solana, Polkadot, and Avalanche) as well as the rise of new layers that reproduce the elements of concentrated finance (loaning, instalments, and commercial centres) or backing fresh out of the plastic new use cases.

The modern world is effectively embracing DeFi, as the previous months have seen an increase in DeFi unicorns - like Anchorage (resource care and administration), Fireblocks (embeddable APIs for token capacity and computerised resource activities), and Lukka (administrative centre stage for DeFi evaluating).

- **DeFi meets Fintech/Insurtech & Vice-a-Versa**

  Laid out Fintechs and Insuretechs are as of now bridling DeFi and bringing its usefulness into their buyer confronting brands. Fintechs have been key drivers in the advancement of banking choices, offering clients better approaches to pay and deal with their cash. Insurtech organisations have done likewise by utilising innovation to present better client encounters. DeFi is following consistent step, particularly on the grounds that Fintechs and insurtech companies can flawlessly mesh DeFi usefulness into their current UIs, making it more agreeable and purchasers well disposed of.

Simultaneously as Fintechs and insuretechs are infringing on DeFi stages by integrating decentralised usefulness into their applications, new DeFi participants are attempting to remove neobanks and challenging guarantors with separated items that influence the blockchain.

For example, a few tasks, including Juno, Dharma, Linen, and Outlet, are sending off DeFi neobanks. They want to give clients high return investment funds that rival cash records of new Fintech companies like Wealthfront and neobanks like Monzo. This is empowered by giving a basic substitute financial point of interaction that consistently mixes crypto and conventional money.

9.5. Web3: It Gets Really Fascinating

2022 onwards, DeFi, Fintech, and insurtech will keep on merging considerably more, posing an existential danger to customary banks and back up plans. The combination of Fintech and Insurtech with DeFi will open considerably more extensive doors beyond the decentralisation of money related streams.

These open doors will be further fuelled by Web3. Utilising blockchain foundation, Web3 can offer open, decentralised information bases and register layers instead of siloed servers or cloud occasions. As clients journey the web and use monetary applications, the information from those corporations no longer exclusively stays on that particular application's server. It is recorded on a common pen record.

Because of open, straightforward exchanges and cooperations, fundamental monetary capabilities, for example, credit scoring, personality confirmation, and misrepresentation counteraction will be reconfigured, bringing about numerous advantages for customers. In particular, Web3 shifts the overall influence back to the purchaser.

The capability of people and organisations to execute things across the globe- - liberated from obstruction by focal groups - makes way for a vigorous financial environment on the web. This is especially outstanding for content and amusement makers, to whom Web3 offers novel and strong ways of interfacing and drawing in with their crowds or fans.

There are likewise benefits for monetary establishments. Think about guarantors. Utilising blockchain's circulated record innovation, safety net providers can store and approach a solitary case's data, refuting the need to put resources into public and confidential spaces.

Blockchain innovation, combined with conveyed record innovation, can likewise help banks diminish or dispose of the utilisation of middle people. Explicit areas in which banks can benefit profoundly from these advances are instalments, freedom and settlement frameworks, raising money, protections, advances and credit, money exchange, client KYC and extortion avoidance.

The monetary administration industry is going through significant disturbances, prodded on by innovation improvements, for example, blockchain and circulated records. What's sure is that DeFi is setting down deep roots, Web3 is not too far off, and monetary administrations won't ever go back.

Monetary foundations, everything being equal, should begin permitting admittance to DeFi usefulness to buyers through their banking and protection administrations. Any other way, they'll be left in the residue by DeFi stages and challengers that see the future — and what's in store mixes usability and accommodation with the force of decentralised finance.

DAPP is the fastest growing usage of the Blockchain and Web3

A DAPP (Decentralised Application) consists of back-end code that runs on a decentralised peer-to-peer network. A DAPP can also have a user interface created by front-end code that makes calls to the back end. DAPPs do not require a central authority to function: they allow for direct interaction between users and providers.

DAPPs often have the following characteristics:

- They run on blockchain
- Their code is made open-source and operates autonomously without any person or group controlling the majority of tokens
- They generate DAPP tokens to provide value to their contributing nodes
- Users are granted access to them in exchange of tokens

- Miners are rewarded with tokens when they successfully contribute to the ecosystem
- Unlike most Apps in use today, DAPPs store all their data on a blockchain and have their back end code running on a blockchain instead of with a central authority.

Ethereum delineates three primary categories of DAPPs:

1. **Money management applications:** users can transact with one another on a blockchain network using its intrinsic currency. These DAPPs usually have their own blockchains, and we often refer to them as cryptocurrencies (such as Bitcoin).
2. **Applications that integrate money with external, real-world events:** for example, a logistics company may use an RFID chip location to determine that a shipment of cargo has reached a port and only then release the payment for the shipment. This could even be accomplished with funds on the blockchain, with no human intervention, if both the buyer and the seller enter into a smart contract.
3. **Decentralised Autonomous Organizations (DAOs):** decentralised, leaderless organisations on the blockchain. These run from conception according to programmatically defined rules about what entities can be members, how members can vote, what businesses or activities they can engage in, and how tokens, funds, or value are exchanged. Once deployed, DAPPs operate autonomously according to their rules. Their members can be geographically dispersed anywhere.

To date, DAPP startups (built on top of blockchain platforms) have constituted the majority of ICOs. Most current Category 2 and Category 3 DAPPs use the Ethereum platform.

DAPPs present a new paradigm for Fintech and money management-related applications.

Why DAPPs?

DAPPs essentially allow all of the back-end code and data to be decentralised and hence immutable and tamperproof. Considering the decentralised nature of these applications coupled with the mechanisms that secure blockchain data, DAPPs have the potential to unlock a diverse array of use cases.

A few benefits of creating a DAPP rather than a normal application include:

- **Payment processing:** No need to integrate with a fiat payment provider to accept funds from users, as users can transact directly using cryptocurrencies.
- **User credentials:** Using a system of public and private keys, users can transact and bind their user sessions and metadata easily and with varying degrees of anonymity, negating the need for lengthy sign-up or registration processes.
- **Trust and auditability:** Open-source DAPP code is accessible and understandable to savvy users. This transparency and the inherent security of the enclosed data generate confidence in the applications. A public record on the blockchain also makes transaction information easy to audit by users or third parties.

9.5.1. CBDC - Key Revolution in Waiting for Global Financial Systems

According to Bank of America's report in Jan 2023, at least 114 central banks—representing 58% of all countries, which generate 95% of global GDP—are now exploring central bank digital currencies (CBDCs), up from 35 in May 2020.

And a team of cryptocurrency analysts from Bank of America is unabashedly bullish on the tech.

Max Koopsen, a member of the content team at crypto exchange OKX, has very insightful comments about the report-relevant highlights are captured here.

"Digital currencies appear inevitable," a new research report from BofA concludes. "We view distributed ledgers and digital currencies, such as CBDCs and stablecoins, as a natural evolution of today's monetary and payment systems."

The report includes analyses of CBDCs' potential benefits and risks—both in their issuance and non-issuance—as well as potential approaches to their distribution. As part of the study, there are also several case studies into CBDC development and challenges within specific economic blocs and nations.

Some key observations from the analysts revolve around the current financial system's antiquated infrastructure and numerous inefficiencies—issues that properly developed CBDCs might solve instantly.

Here's a look at CBDCs' benefits for banks and the unbanked-

1. CBDCs' potential to remove intermediaries—once technology makes them redundant—could bring about real-time settlement, complete transparency, and lower costs, the report states.
2. The analysts point to an estimated $4 trillion of capital that banks are required to deposit in corresponding banks in order to remove settlement risk. The study argues that this is an inefficient capital allocation that could otherwise be generating yield elsewhere.
3. Furthermore, less capitalised banks and payment service providers cannot expand into cross-border payments, the research report argues, partly due to the requirement to pre-fund accounts at correspondent banks: "In reality, cross-border payments are routed through 2.6 different correspondent banks on an average, increasing time for settlement," the report notes. "However, 20% of euro-denominated cross-border payments require the involvement of 5 + correspondent banks." The result? Cross-border payments cost ten times more than domestic payments.
4. The researchers also predict that CBDC adoption will positively impact the unbanked population, which is 1.4 billion people worldwide, and 6.5% of the U.S. population, according to 2021 figures from the U.S. Federal Reserve.
5. The unbanked cannot access standard financial services nor have pathways to building their credit history. As a result, they face increased separation from their wealth,

e.g. reliance on payday-loan services that offer only subpar terms and conditions.

6. If a CBDC wallet was developed to fulfil basic financial services such as being able to hold, send, and receive funds, as well as establishing credit histories and providing credit scores, this disparity could be almost entirely eliminated.

CBDCs vs. stablecoins—fight!

This is certainly no less a battle than the battle of the Titans, where each entity seems to be determined to win. However, the truth is that the real winner in any such battle is the consumer who gets the best of both worlds. Let's view this battle up close and center from our first-row seats.

1. The report also includes a few words about the role stablecoins could play in CBDC adoption. Noting the significant growth in stablecoin transaction volumes over the past two years—which reached $7.9 trillion in 2022.
2. "The proliferation of stablecoins for cross-border and domestic payments and transfers could inhibit a central bank's ability to implement monetary policy if growth remains unchecked and unregulated, as well as increase systemic risk," the report's authors state. "In some cases, loss of monetary control could lead to inflation, significantly above current central bank targets."
3. Because their controls still perform favourably compared to some traditional financial systems, the analysts say they

"expect stablecoin adoption and use for payments to increase in the absence of CBDCs as financial institutions explore digital asset custody and trading solutions."

4. Should issuing a CBDC take too long, however, the researchers worry that stablecoins could proliferate even further into cross-border and even domestic payments. Allowing stablecoins to become entrenched will "increase systemic risk in the traditional market and impede a central bank's ability to implement monetary policy."
5. The report does entertain a future in which both stablecoins and CBDCs can coexist. According to the analysts, stablecoins will likely continue to excel in certain use cases, especially when smart contracts are involved. However, just a few lines later, the researchers suggest that stablecoins are not fit for this world.
6. "CBDCs' design and programmability will likely determine the level of future stablecoin adoption and usage," the report states. "We also note that the potential for CBDCs to displace stablecoins largely depends on the former being interoperable with blockchains and blockchain-based applications."

CBDCs' Risks for Banks and Privacy:

1. After six pages exploring the potential benefits of CBDCs, the Bank of America analysts turn to the potential risks of issuing and not issuing CBDCs. Topping the list of risks: the potential competition between commercial banks, such as Bank of America, and the central bank.

According to the analysts, "CBDCs are in some ways superior to bank accounts as stores of value, particularly during times of crisis."

2. Though commercial banks and central banks currently exist in a two-tier system, CBDCs could blur the demarcation lines, according to the report. If commercial banks' customers are able to swiftly and easily transfer their savings out of a commercial bank and into the central bank, how would the commercial bank be able to continue borrowing and lending their customers' funds?
3. Indeed, the analysts' second-ranked risk is that bank runs could occur more frequently if safeguards are not included in the CBDC's design.
4. "During times of stress in the banking system, people could withdraw deposits and exchange them for CBDCs, given that there is no credit or liquidity risk if distributed with direct and hybrid approaches, increasing financial stability risks," they write.
5. Apart from the potential collapse of the commercial banking industry, the researchers grapple with two important questions: How will governments convince their citizens to use its CBDC? And what will governments be capable of if and when they do? Large-scale policy rollouts will almost certainly be piecemeal, the analysts concede, prone to gaffes and marred by controversy.

Eleven countries have already issued CBDCs, and the largest central banks around the world are either exploring designs or launching pilots.

According to the analysts, the first CBDCs were designed mainly for retail banking use and were issued by the central banks of developing economies in an attempt to broaden financial inclusion in the absence of a commercial banking sector.

However, the Eastern Caribbean Central Bank's CBDC, one of the 11 first-generation attempts, faced a crippling setback after the platform crashed in January 2022 and was unable to facilitate transactions for two months.

Adoption and usage of the ECCB's CBDC have been "largely uninspiring so far," according to the analysts.

Central banks are no doubt paying attention to the successes and failures of this inaugural class of CBDCs. Meanwhile, as central banks and governments are preparing for the launch of next-gen CBDCs, Bank of America analysts worry that mainstream adoption of CBDCs could face backlash over privacy concerns.

Potential headwinds to CBDC adoption could result from the loss of privacy and anonymity that the public enjoys with physical cash, the authors concede. For this, the analysis suggests a policy-based compromise.

"Payments using CBDCs can remain anonymous if a legal framework exists providing a central bank or government the right to trace transactions if there are indications of criminal activity, tax evasion, money laundering or terrorism financing," they write. "But purely anonymous payments are anathema to central banks."

However, the researchers go on to emphasise that any perceived or legitimate invasions of privacy might push the public to reevaluate the policy initiative and possibly result in higher demand for CBDCs with stronger legal protections.

9.5.2. NFTs - Non Fungible Tokens

An NFT is a unique digital asset that can be bought or sold. Its definition is captured in the name itself: NFT is an abbreviation for a "non-fungible token."

If something is non-fungible, it is unique or irreplaceable. A good example here is a mass-produced postcard of the "Mona Lisa" is fungible, whereas the original "Mona Lisa" is non-fungible.

One of the reasons why NFTs can be hard to define is because any digital file can become one—from songs, artwork and clothing to tickets, memes, video clips and more. As a result, NFTs have ignited discussions around what it means to value and own digital items, not the least for the potential financial gain to be had from creating and selling them.

The world of NFTs isn't without its challenges, though.

Most NFTs are currently stored on an open-source blockchain called Ethereum—a kind of online public blockchain record that keeps track of who owns what. As well as concerns over theft, plagiarism and fakes, or the gender disparity within the space itself.

9.6 DLT - Distributed Ledger Technology

Distributed ledgers are interconnected systems that enable the untrusting participants to form and maintain consensus about the existence, status and evolution of a shared block of information.

Typical Attributes of Distributed Ledgers are:

- **Cryptography:** Strong cryptography is used to authenticate access to each block of information.
- **Immutable Information/Non-Repudiation:** Built-in mechanism to preserve the integrity of the block of information as well as the audit trail of access and changes to the information.
- **Smart Contracts:** Already covered in the sessions - these are used for automatic execution of the business logic when a certain business scenario is triggered or a state criterion is met.
- **Shared Ledger:** The Block of transaction ledger information is shared across the participants and updated in real time as agreed with a pre-decided mechanism. Also, access to this information is based on the permissions given.
- **Distributed Consensus:** As mentioned about the shared ledger, the truth or the state of information is represented by the consensus of the participating stakeholders

9.7.Applying Decentralised Finance to Business Scenarios

9.7.1. Decentralised Banks (R3 Corda, Onyx by JPM)

According to the R3 Corda website, David E. Rutter and Todd McDonald founded R3 in 2014 with the belief that direct, digital collaboration is the future for highly regulated industries everywhere.

With R3's beginnings as a consortium backed by over 60 banks, they knew first-hand that there was a lack of trust in how financial institutions collaborate and transact with each other. They believed that if these organisations were less centralised and more connected through the use of blockchain technology and other multi-party trust technology, then entire industries could collaborate in ways they never thought possible. With a passion to drive this vision forward, R3 developed Corda—a purpose-built DLT application development platform that has facilitated hundreds of blockchain applications and networks across banking, capital markets, global trade, insurance and beyond.

Essentially R3's Corda is a permission-based private distributed ledger technology.

The key differences between R3's Corda and public blockchain are as follows.

1. It is blockchain-inspired but not actually blockchain-based. Instead, it is a private permissioned distributed ledger.
2. **Enterprise Grade:** Although an open community-based R3 Corda is available from 2022. The Enterprise version is the high-grade version specifically built for the financial markets like banks, and insurance.
3. **Data Privacy:** Privacy of the data is at the core of the Corda network. The transactions are only accessible if

permitted. For example, a network of ten banks, each represented by a node, may exchange a block of information over the network and also interact directly with one another in a private mode. If two banks intend to transact directly with each other but want to keep the data involved in the transaction confidential, they can do so privately, a feature supported by Enterprise Corda.

4. **Consensus:** In Corda, the consensus is at a transaction level and not at the system level. There are multiple mechanisms supported for consensus. The notary is Corda's unique consensus service. It ensures each transaction contains only unique input states. A notary service is formed by one or more notary workers that together form a notary cluster. The notary's role is to ensure a transaction contains only unique input states

5. **Regulatory Focus:** The Corda Network enables Observer nodes. Posting transactions to an observer node is a common requirement in finance, where regulators often want to receive comprehensive reporting on all actions taken. By running their own node, regulators can receive a stream of digitally signed, de-duplicated reports useful for later processing.

6. **Faster Operation:** Efficiency and speed of operations are extremely important for financial Institutions. One disadvantage of many public blockchains, particularly those based on the Proof of Work (PoW) verification model, is the slow speed of transaction verification. Corda's advantage over these public blockchains is a much faster

transaction verification. While Bitcoin (BTC) or Ethereum (ETH) can take several minutes, sometimes up to a few hours, to verify a transaction, on Corda, it could take mere seconds, depending on the complexity of the private network involved.

7. **Easy Integration:** Reusing existing skills is possible to build integration with bank systems. Query & joins to existing DBs with SQL and code contract in Java enables this.

Italian Banks Integrate Corda

According to multiple news outlets, in a bid to drastically reduce the time required to complete interbank data transfers and simultaneously ensure frictionless operations, a vast array of lenders under the Italian Banking Association (Associazione Bancaria Italiana or ABI) are now using Spunta, a distributed ledger technology solution powered by R3's Corda. As per sources close to the matter, in the existing system, reconciliation and interbank transfers took between 30 to 50 days to complete and it was largely unpredictable.

However, with the new Spunta blockchain solution, reconciliation is done within 24 hours, says Silvia Attanasio, head of innovation at ABI.

Notably, the Corda-based Spunta system was designed by NTT Data, an information technology firm and it's operated by SIA, a bank technology firm.

The team says the integration of blockchain technology was necessitated by the updated Interbank Agreement, which went live in May 2019.

Another Banking decentralised solution is Onyx by J.P. Morgan. This is at the forefront of a major shift in the financial services industry. JPM offers a blockchain-based platform for wholesale payments transactions, helping to re-architect the way that money, information and assets are moving around the world. This is an upcoming solution from JPM.

Onyx is pioneering the world's first blockchain-based platform for wholesale payment transactions, helping to transform the way that money, information and assets are moving around the world.

9.7.2. Decentralised Wealthtech-Digitised Blockchain Bonds

Digitised blockchain bonds are a type of bond that is issued and traded on a blockchain network.

This is a typical application of Decentralised Wealth management that is issued by reputed financial institutions. A digitised bond is recorded on a distributed ledger, which makes it more secure and transparent than traditional bonds.

Digitised blockchain bonds can offer a number of advantages over traditional bonds, as any other blockchain-based distributed ledger system.

1. **Increased security:** The distributed ledger technology used by digitised blockchain bonds makes them more secure than traditional bonds. This is because the data is stored on multiple computers, so it is not possible for one computer to hack or corrupt the entire system.

2. **Transparency:** The distributed ledger technology used by digitised blockchain bonds also makes them more transparent than traditional bonds. This is because all of the transactions are recorded on the ledger, so anyone can see how the bond is performing.
3. **Efficiency:** Digitised blockchain bonds can be more efficient than traditional bonds. This is because the transactions can be processed more quickly and easily on the blockchain network.
4. **Cost-effectiveness:** Digitised blockchain bonds can be more cost-effective than traditional bonds. This is because the blockchain network eliminates the need for intermediaries, such as brokers and clearinghouses.

However, as with everything else, there are some disadvantages and risks as well:

1. **Complexity:**

   The distributed ledger technology used by digitised blockchain bonds can be complex, which may make it difficult for some investors to understand.
2. **Regulation:**

   The regulatory environment for digitised blockchain bonds is still evolving, which may create uncertainty for some investors.
3. **Lack of liquidity:**

   The market for digitised blockchain bonds is still relatively small, which may make it difficult to trade these bonds.

Summary

Decentralised Financed has been experiencing prolific growth in the past year. As we have seen in this chapter various mechanisms and tools have been developed to fulfil DeFi promise as a dis-intermediated financial ecosystem. Decentralisation has distinct advantages over traditional finance in terms of Transparency and Innovation opportunity. The blockchain along with smart contracts has been the most widely used decentralisation approached as we have reviewed in details. We have also looked at the countries considering CBDC as the future central banking using blockchain. The financial world has various reservations about the decentralised financing because of the tectonic shift in the governance model as compared to the traditional models. The chapter also covers very specific implementations of such as NFT - non fungible tokens, R3 Corda as the blockchain platform. There are specific implementations of these platforms for Insurance and health management sectors. Overall the decentralise finance model is still in its infancy and there are multitude of opportunities of researching and innovating.

Designing financial solutions entails refining human behaviour.

Chapter 10

Disruptions - Focused Financing

10.1. E-RUPI

As the name makes clear, the e-RUPI voucher is a virtual payment voucher that provides ease of transaction without actually exchanging physical currency.

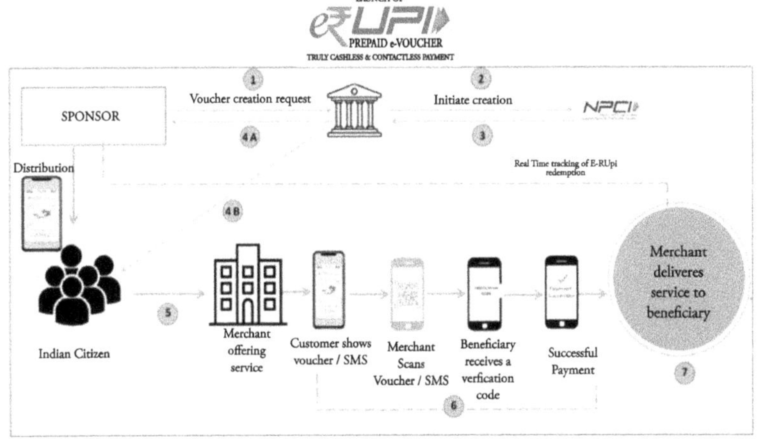

The above flow diagram shows in detail the concept, components, mechanism& working of an e-RUPI.

So, let us discuss in detail what is an e-RUPI Prepaid Voucher.

- The idea behind an e-RUPI is to create a minimal logistics, leak-proof delivery mechanism for a wide range of government Direct Benefit Transfer (DBT) programs across the country.
- The e-RUPI voucher is allowed to be redeemed for P2M purchases only
- It is a QR code or SMS string-based e-voucher, which is sent to the beneficiaries mobile
- Its Usage is restricted to specific persons and product/ services only (MCC code & a Purpose Code Mapper is used)
- No Mobile Application required by/for the beneficiary
- The e-RUPI voucher can be created or revoked on the request of the Sponsor (Government/Private Entities)
- The e-RUPI voucher has a predefined expiry (1 year)
- Typical usages to start with include: students for a Scholarship program, payment of utility bills, medical facilities, to buy agricultural products like fertilisers, etc...
- There is no prerequisite for a beneficiary to avail e-RUPI, i.e., e-RUPI does not require the customer to have a bank account etc.
- It ensures an easy, contactless, two-step redemption process that does not require sharing of personal details either.

10.2 Disrupting e-Commerce (ONDC)

This is India's Initiative for Open e-Commerce: Open Network for Digital Commerce.

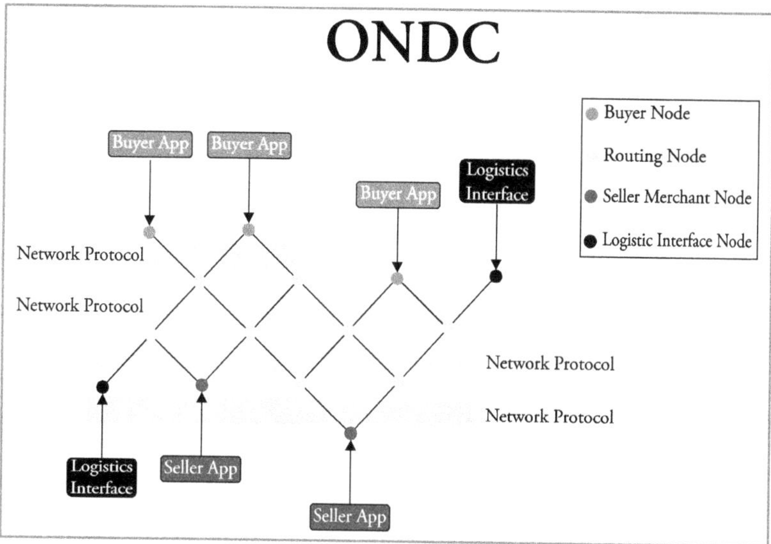

The above figure shows how ONDC- Open Network Digital Commerce works by interfacing the buyer & seller Apps. Let us explore this in detail below.

In this digital commerce world, accelerating growth is vital. People who plan to set up a digital e-commerce platform should know that putting diverse elements together and working towards making every element a success is very important.

Open Network for Digital Commerce or ONDC allows you to grow and succeed via e-commerce by connecting with network partners competing with your digital commerce solutions.

What is Open Network for Digital Commerce or ONDC?

Open Network for Digital Commerce has been established as an alternative to online platform aggregators that are said to monopolise the e-commerce landscape.

ONDC is also referred to as a network of various large and small-scale online and offline traders. Though this is still in a growing phase, ONDC is being pitched as one of the effective solutions to break the monopoly and dominance of large e-commerce firms.

ONDC is seen as an important step towards making e-commerce processes open-source, creating a platform that all online vendors and retailers can use.

This great initiative promotes open platforms for all aspects of exchanging services and goods via electronic networks.

The ONDC network is based on open protocols and allows even local commerce across segments like food orders, mobility, travel bookings, and more to be connected by any network-enabled application.

- **How did the Concept Come into Existence?**

  ONDC was conceptualised based on objectives such as:

  - Curbing digital monopolies,
  - Supporting small and medium enterprises,
  - Helping small traders easily get on online platforms
  - Creating new opportunities.

ONDC is the first initiative to democratise and incorporate digital commerce, shifting from a platform-centric model to an open-network model.

ONDC will allow local sellers and buyers to be visible and transact digitally through open networks regardless of the application or platform used. The idea is to help even the small local sellers and buyers to create an identity on the e-platform and perform their business. The concept behind ONDC includes helping small sellers and buyers in creating an identity on the e-platform and being able to do their business.

ONDC came into existence to empower consumers and merchants by breaking the dominance and creating a single network to drive, scale and innovate, thus transforming businesses. This is expected to digitise the supply chain, provide logistics, standardise operations and offer value for consumers. This integrated platform will also enable businesses to list their products for sale digitally.

- **How does ONDC Work?**

  In ONDC, there are many platforms where sellers can take their products and get access to suppliers that will be connected to the network. Hence, find the best prices for their supplies through ONDC and get a host of reliable digital tools.

- **How is ONDC Beneficial to Sellers?**

  Sellers will get a host of digital transformation tools to get their business online. They can accomplish this even without being affiliated with an e-commerce company and wouldn't be bound by any predatory commissions. Sellers can also connect to a wide array of inventor supplies, therefore, giving supplies to choose from.

- **How is ONDC Beneficial to Buyers?**

  Reports reveal that buyers would get ONDC as a democratised platform, free from private e-commerce platforms' regulated prices. Moreover, buyers won't be limited to ordering services and products only from huge companies and can connect with small and local businesses or stores as well.

- **Advantages of ONDC When You Own an e-commerce Platform**

  Digital commerce is rapidly growing and is expected to proliferate continuously in the coming days. ONDC is something that people who own e-commerce platforms should take advantage of during this digital commerce boom. The advantages of ONDC, when you own an e-Ccommerce platform, are as follows:

  - **Break the walls among sellers and purchasers/consumers:** The huge online business players have periods of health crisis and have created a competitive slope. Be that as it may, ONDC tends to democratise the uneven market landscape by freeing the platform-centric model and establishing a seller-buyer-centric platform.
  - **Sustain people's modern needs and ensure convenience:** The need for ONDC is of great importance: Don't miss out on the trend and the competition. Established

restaurants take WhatsApp bookings and orders through telephone calls and do not lose even one selling space. You can certainly consider reaping enormous benefits and profits if you board your organisation or business on Open Network for Digital Commerce.

- **Connect with your clients from numerous platforms:** Who would want to ignore the immense multi-channel shopper crowd? From providing low buyer-finder pay to allowing freedom, ONDC frees organisations from hefty commission rates. In this scenario, you set the costs for your clients without intermediaries.
- **A platform that guarantees low investment:** ONDC is a low-investment platform that you should try. ONDC demands a minimal expense of client acquisition, with just the purchaser-finder fee and zero web-based selling expenses. The service cost is decreased with the personal and 3rd-party logistic choices. Aside from the expanded local visibility, Open Network for Digital Commerce gets rid of the cost of digital marketing, with apps being the regular customers.

Your customer base couldn't imagine anything better than to purchase from and do business with you on web-based spaces. What's more, if you intend to go online, now is the best time to get to the platform and perform better to reach or even exceed expectations.

Nowadays, people with a Google Pay account can transfer money to other people using mobile phones that are both using the Unified Payments Interface or UPI platform. Governments are now planning the same experiment in the digital commerce space that Flipkart and Amazon presently dominate. Open Network for Digital Commerce, or ONDC, promises to give a playing field to small sellers or merchants too. This is believed to move eCommerce away from the present platform-centric models.

ONDC will completely change this scenario. This will not just be an e-commerce platform and website to sell or purchase products. ONDC will be a network wherein different buyers, sellers, and delivery partners will register themselves. This will also be a well-established connection between all entities and bodies. Therefore, a cross-connection will be guaranteed to introduce a more centralised and broader marketplace. Launching ONDC will provide people with a platform that works seamlessly and provides superior alternatives to sellers and consumers.

10.3 Disrupting Lending (OCEN)

- **Pronounced as O-KEN**

  OCEN (Open Credit Enablement Network) is the new disruption on the Indian Fintech scene.

  Like the UPI payments revolutionised digital payments in India, OCEN (or Open Credit Enablement Network) is going to transform credit infrastructure that allows applicants to connect with lenders with zero baggage.

- **What is this OCEN (Open Credit Enablement Network)?**

  OCEN (Open Credit Enablement Network) is a new ecosystem which aims to bring financial products to: MSMEs (Micro, Small & Medium Enterprises) and Individuals.

  The goal is to democratise access to the credit system in India.

  OCEN has built an ecosystem to enable service providers to become fully-fledged, fintech-enabled credit marketplaces.

  Every startup in India can eventually become a fintech startup. That's the power of OCEN. This is going to boost the "Make In India" Initiative multifold.

10.4. SuperApps

SuperApps are the future - we will be seeing more and more SuperApps over the next couple of years. It will not be a surprise if we see the year 2023 as the year of SuperApps.

Let us take a reference App here as an example. The largest SuperApp used in the world today is WeChat by Tencent. The following picture depicts the WeChat SuperApp model and its capabilities in clear detail.

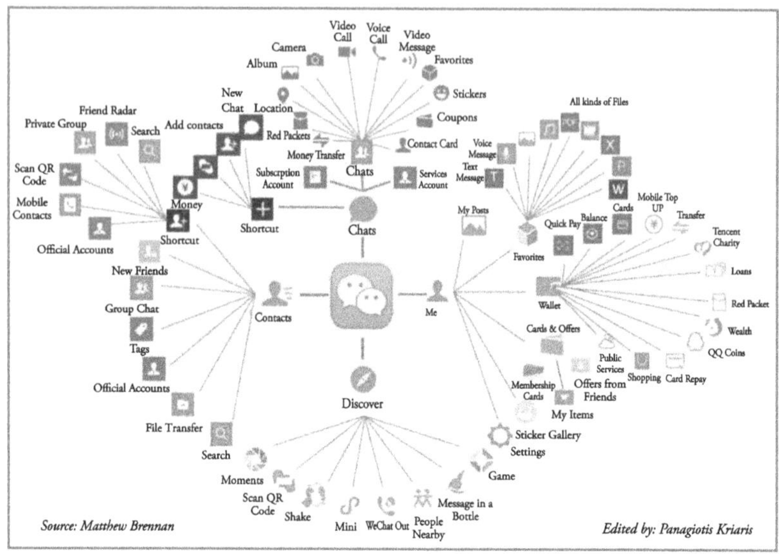

But here, you might wonder, what is a Super app?

According to Gartner, the definition of a super app is

"An App that provides end-users (customers, partners or employees) with a set of core features plus access to independently created mini-apps."

They deliver a mobile-first experience that truly caters to a growing digital-native generation. Gartner compares SuperApps with Swiss army knives, supporting many multiple-purpose tools though ultimately creating an overall better, more bespoke user experience based on preferences and usage.

Superapps can consolidate and replace multiple apps for customer or employee use and support a composable business ecosystem. According to Gartner, 50% of the world population would be active daily on multiple SuperApps by 2027.

Gartner recently published their 2023 trends report, which highlights major technology initiatives to look for in the next year. If you're not using superapps yet, you might be missing out on a major avenue for adding business value and improving your mobile user experience.

The figure below details the typical architecture of a SuperApp showing how it integrates all the apps into a single user interface.

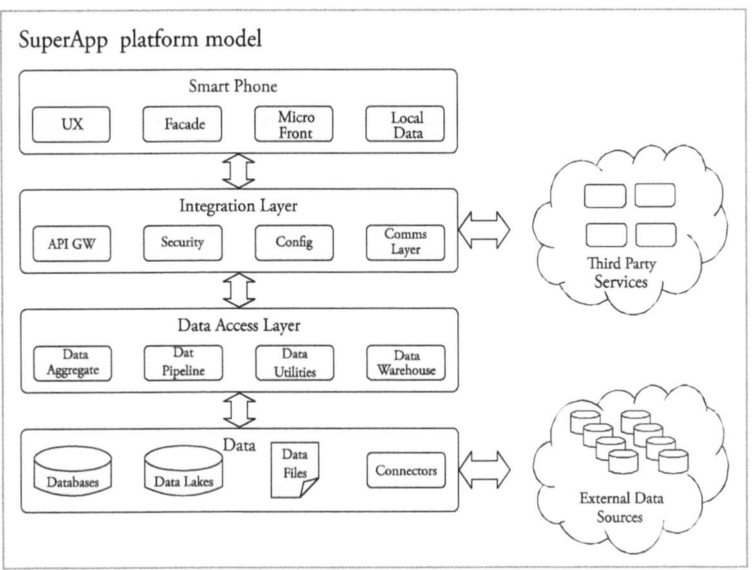

The top SuperApps to watch out for in the year 2023 are:

1. WeChat
2. Amazon
3. TataNeu
4. AliPay
5. Revolute

6. PhonePe
7. Grab

10.5 Fintech Coopetition (Co-operative Competition)

As discussed earlier in 3.2.1 cooperative-competition is a business strategy in which organisations cooperate with each other in some areas while competing with each other in other areas.

This can be a beneficial strategy for organisations, as it allows them to share resources and expertise while also driving innovation and growth.

There are many different examples of cooperative competition in the business world.

For example, two organisations might collaborate on research and development, while competing in the marketplace for sales.

Or, two organisations might cooperate on supply chain management while competing in the marketplace for customers.

Cooperative competition can be a successful strategy for businesses of all sizes. However, it is important to carefully consider the specific competitive landscape and the potential benefits and risks of collaboration before entering into any partnerships.

The advantages of cooperative competition can be summarised:

1. **Increased innovation:** By cooperating with each other, organisations can work together on ideas and share expertise, which can lead to new and innovative products and services.

2. **Improved efficiency:** By cooperating in areas such as supply chain management and marketing, companies can reduce costs and improve efficiency.
3. **Increased market share:** By cooperating on sales and distribution, organisations can reach a wider audience and increase their market share.
4. **Enhanced customer service:** By cooperating on customer service, organisations can provide a better experience for their customers.
5. **Strengthened relationships:** By cooperating with each other, organisations can build stronger relationships with their partners, which can lead to future opportunities for cooperation.

However, organisations need to be aware of certain risk statements as well when they are cooperating and collaborating.

1. **Loss of competitive advantage:** If organisations share too much specific information with their partners, they may lose their competitive advantage.
2. **Increased artificial dependency:** If organisations become too dependent on their partners, they may be vulnerable to disruptions in the supply chain or changes in the market.
3. **Dispute resolution becomes detrimental to growth:** disagreements arise between partners, and they may be difficult to resolve due to interdependence.

4. **Increased risk of collusion:** If organisations collaborate too closely, they may be accused of collusion, which is illegal in some countries.

Generally, cooperative competition can be considered a beneficial strategy for businesses if conducted in a very careful and diligent manner before entering into the collaboration.

In the Fintech ecosystem following are typical examples by which Fintech organisations are cooperating and competing in the marketplace at the same time.

The typical cooperation between Fintech companies is in the following two areas:

- **Technology:** Building innovative technology by joining forces. That can be applied specifically to individual products
- **Regulatory:** In the subsequent sections the regulatory requirements of Fintech are discussed, saying that this is a very strong area where Fintech companies work together to formulate and enhance the regulatory ecosystem with a goal of offering more secured products to the consumer.

Notable examples in very recent times which exhibit this phenomenon of cooperation and competition at the same time are.

1. **Visa and Master Card: Cooperate on blockchain technology:** Visa and Mastercard are both investing in blockchain technology, which is a distributed ledger technology that can be used to record financial transactions.

They are cooperating on ways to use blockchain technology to improve the efficiency and security of payments. At the same time, both of these organisations are strong competitors in the financial marketplace as payment brands. Visa and MasterCard both also cooperate together on the security regulations like PCI and EMV - Euro MasterCard Visa - secure credit card initiative.

2. **Ant Financial and SoftBank:** are strong competitors in mobile payment and providing financial services like investments, loans and insurance on mobile phones. They are investing heavily in payment companies, like Ant financials as Alibaba's parent company is a major investor in a number of Fintech companies, including Affirm, Credit Karma, and SoFi. SoftBank is also a major investor in a number of Fintech companies, including Lemonade, MoneyLion, and Remitly. Both companies are trying to gain an edge in the Fintech industry by investing in promising startups. At the same time, they are cooperating on developing new-age Mobile Payment platforms that can work in China and Japan and also could be expanded across the world.

10.6. Metaverse

Metaverse is one of the latest tech stacks. The Fintech sector will be impacted by using these new virtual reality tools and technologies provided by Metaverse. The financial sector, including banking and other industries, is building solutions for Metaverse.

Metaverse represents the next stage of evolution in the banking and Fintech industry, offering customers the experience of virtual banking. In a sense, one can say that the metaverse allows for the return of personalised banking with the help of virtual or augmented reality (VR/AR). It is expected that the majority of banks globally will be using AR/VR as an alternative channel for customer transactions as well as for employee engagement.

Metaverse gained much attention in October when social media giant Facebook changed its name to Meta. A parcel of real estate on the virtual reality platform Decentraland was recently sold for $2.4 million, and Republic Realm paid $4.3 million for a property in The Sandbox metaverse in early 2022. The Bank of America strategist also predicted that traditional payments companies will be much more interested in cryptocurrencies if they become widely used in Metaverse.

Earlier in 2022, global investment bank Morgan Stanley said that the metaverse is the next big investment theme. Last week, Grayscale Investments published a report stating that the metaverse is potentially a $1 trillion business opportunity. Recently Goldman Sachs indicated that Metaverse could generate $3 trillion in annual economic activity by 2030. The report suggests that Metaverse will create new revenue streams for companies across various industries, including financial services and banking.

Key FinTech Leadership Talking Points on Metaverse Opportunity

Currently, there are no obvious killer applications for Metaverse, and no one knows when or how they will evolve. One thing everyone agrees on is this: they do not want to be caught flat-footed.

Most Metaverse users are going to be Generations Z and Alpha. To acquire these customer bases, many organisations are in the process of creating engaging experiences. Persuading this group to 'invest' in virtual assets, and to insure and trade them, requires the development of a foundational Metaverse culture. Trying to impose physical-world constructs on Metaverse may or may not work. For example, a Metaverse ATM might be a good idea by offering a familiar metaphor for deposits, withdrawals, and currency exchanges. However, a virtual insurance broker might not go over as well (or vice versa).

So, here's a blue-print for navigating the Metaverse by being prepared.

- **Plan for scarce talent and resources.**

  Skilled resources will be in short supply and hot demand, so companies must be thoughtful about acquiring and developing the required skill sets or identifying partners who can help. Predictably, as Metaverse takes off, designers and engineers skilled in Metaverse technologies and culture will be in high demand and short supply. This happened for Web 1.0, Web 2.0, and the initial phases of the smartphone revolution, as well.

- **Examine your new products and services with a Metaverse lens.**

  Innovators must think outside the box about the new products and services Metaverse will demand and enable. While it was evident from the outset of Web 2.0 that even non-technical end users could now remotely author web content, few of us thought there would be 600 million blogs worldwide and 31 million active bloggers in the US alone. Picture-, video-, and voice-oriented remotely authored, interactive sites such as Instagram and TikTok have over a billion users each!

- **Prepare to work through being an outlier in your organisation.**

  Anticipate that your new sources of revenue using emerging technologies will start out small and may come under pressure in your company. Be ready. 'Simple' things like accepting micropayments or handling virtual transactions may cause a backlash. Because no one knows if and when this technology will catch on, you must either be comfortable taking the risk ahead of the curve, have a plan to catch up with your own technology or wait until Metaverse is established and acquires a successful player – probably at a very high valuation.

- **How will virtual experiences coexist alongside – and even complement – traditional ones?**

  If you are a current bank or insurance provider, be ready to support a dual business model and pay attention to the emerging competition. Don't underestimate the impact on banks in terms of launching virtual or "banks of the future" in Metaverse. Insurance companies could open virtual brokerages to assist people choose the right policies, for example. Ensure your strategy incorporates how you will support digital currencies. Speculation in virtual 'equities',' art, 'items of value', and currency arbitrage will certainly see cycles of boom and bust – just like we see in the real world. Have a plan for cryptocurrencies (and even some of the more esoteric currencies of Metaverse, such as Robux) that could be transacted through banks or Metaverse ATMs. Be ready to embrace this experience while preserving the traditional models, as well.

- **Stay agile for first-mover advantages as opportunities arise**

  Pay attention to emerging business models as they are unveiled. Paper-driven processes such as KYC (know your customer) or FNOL (first notice of loss) could be transformed through Metaverse. With 2D technologies, these processes are best at capturing some elements of the real world; with 3D technologies, these could leapfrog a financial institution in its ability to interact – especially with its younger customers.

Summary

In this chapter we have see latest disruptions. India has been at the forefront of the Digital transformation of the Fintech ecosystem. This started with using UPI for Person to Person money transfer or Person to Business money transfer it is using the same payment rails. UPI make a big mark on the world map as India has become the largest processor of digital payments in the world by a very large margin. Also latest financial inclusion initiatives like E-RUPI for agri-fintech sector, E-Commerce framework introduction using ONDC and the most recent OCEN for micro-lending. World has been also moving in fast lane of Fintech. The likes of Metaverse introducing payments in the virtual world. Also all the Big Techs and TechFins are jumping on to the bandwagon of SuperApps. SuperApps is still the area which is untapped. Just as an example I just bought a new car and during the delivery of the car the executive asked me to install at least three applications doing different integrations that would enable me to use the car features optimally. This is bound to change as we have seen in the SuperApps section of the chapter. Consumers do not want to install multiple applications they want one stop shop so it is our responsibility as the technology enablers to hide the integration complexity with the best in class UI/UX experience hiding all the complexity of integration from the consumer. This would include features Fintech features as well. Taking example of Car Maintenance - The toll payment, other bill payments, Fuel payments Electronic Card Charging payments should be accommodated in the SuperApp.

"Human inclinations towards uncovering flaws in the financial system necessitates the implementation of regulatory safeguards, cultivating a just and equitable financial environment."

Chapter 11

Directive Regulatory

11.1. RegTech

Regulatory Compliance in today's corporate world has become most significant in recent times.

Regulatory Compliance means to check whether an organisation complies with the regulations applicable to it. Nowadays the scope of Regulatory Compliance is rising due to an increase in the number of frauds and non-compliance violations.

Riskpro which leads the Regulatory Technology movement in India has designed multiple tools to assist a number of constituents.

Financial Institutions are bearing huge monetary losses due to a growing demand for compliant transactions. Recently Credit Suisse paid $30 Million to settle FCPA offences. Companies are bearing huge costs for compliance procedures. So in recent times, a new concept of Regtech (Regulatory Technology) has come into the limelight.

Regtech means to develop a product which uses Information Technology and aids financial institutions to enhance their regulatory processes.

Regtech is now an emerging field because of many benefits like-

- Low-cost compliance process
- Combating Money Laundering
- Avoidance of non-compliance costs like huge fines
- Efficient compliance management
- Improvement in Corporate Governance
- Transparency in Transactions
- Improving the data quality

Besides these Regtech solutions are agile, fast and speedy and help to create a simple solution for complex data. It is a technology that allows firms to easily adapt to the pressure of increasing regulatory requirements while being cost-effective and secure. This technology will allow companies to automate the process of monitoring data and ease the reporting process to regulatory bodies.

11.2. Technology Doing More Harm than Good?

Fintech as we have seen in earlier sections is a very data-centric industry. At the same time, there is a need to provide services specific to consumer situations and needs. Walking this fine line between providing services with ease & speed while maintaining safety and privacy is a real challenge.

1. **Loss of privacy:** Fintech companies often collect a large amount of data about their users, which could be used to track their spending habits, location, and other personal information. This data could be used for marketing purposes or even sold to third parties.
2. **Increased fraud:** Fintech companies are often targeted by fraudsters, who use sophisticated techniques to steal money from users. This is a growing problem, as Fintech companies become more popular. Fintech companies may not offer the same level of consumer protection as traditional financial institutions. This would make consumers more vulnerable to fraud.
3. **Financial exclusion:** Fintech companies may not be accessible to everyone, especially those who do not have access to the internet or smartphones. This could lead to financial exclusion for some people.
4. **Lack of regulation:** Fintech companies are often subject to less regulation than traditional financial institutions. This can make it more difficult for consumers to get their money back if they are scammed or their data is compromised.

11.3. GDPR

GDPR: General Data Protection Regulation, is a set of rules in the European Union (EU) that gives individuals more control over their personal data.

- **The Need for GDPR**

Increasing amount of personal data that is being collected and processed by organisations.. This data can be used for a variety of purposes, including marketing, advertising, and fraud as we have seen in the earlier session. The GDPR aims to protect individuals from the misuse of their personal data by giving them more control over how their data is collected, used, and shared.

- **How is it regulating Fintech?**

The GDPR also aims to create a more uniform regulatory environment for organisations that process the personal data of individuals in the EU. This is important because it can help to reduce the compliance burden for organisations that operate in multiple EU member states.

The GDPR is a complex regulation, but it is important for organisations that process the personal data of individuals in the EU, to understand and comply with its requirements. Failure to comply with the GDPR can result in significant fines.

The key aspects of GDPR are:

1. **Protecting individual privacy:** GDPR gives individuals more control over their personal data, including the right to access their data, the right to have their data erased, and the right to object to the processing of their data.
2. **Creating a more uniform regulatory environment:** GDPR creates a single set of rules for organisations that process the personal data of individuals in the EU. This can help to reduce the compliance burden for organisations that operate in multiple EU member states.

3. **Promoting innovation:** GDPR allows organisations to use personal data in new and innovative ways, as long as they do so in a way that respects individual privacy.
4. **Protecting businesses from data breaches:** The GDPR requires organisations to take steps to protect personal data from unauthorised access, use, or disclosure. This can help to protect businesses from financial and reputational damage that can result from a data breach.

To Summarise,

GDPR is a comprehensive regulation that aims to protect individual privacy and promote innovation. Organisations that process the personal data of individuals in the EU should take steps to understand and comply with the GDPR's requirements.

11.4 GDPR Outside the European Union

As discussed above GDPR is a regulation applied in the European Union. There are similar security standards introduced in other areas of the world.

The notable standards are as follows:

- **The United States:** The California Consumer Privacy Act (CCPA) is a law that gives consumers in California more control over their personal data. It is similar to the GDPR in many respects, but it also has specific differences and unique provisions, like a requirement for businesses to provide consumers with a way to opt out of the sale of their personal data.

- **India:** The Personal Data Protection Bill, 2021 is a proposed law that would protect the personal data of individuals in India. It is similar to GDPR in the majority of the areas with some differences, such as a requirement for organisations to obtain consent from individuals before collecting or using their personal data for certain purposes, such as marketing.
- **The United Kingdom:** The Data Protection Act 2018 is a law that protects the personal data of individuals in the UK. On top of GDPR, there is an additional requirement for organisations to conduct data protection impact assessments (DPIAs) for certain types of processing activities related to consumer data.
- China has a data protection law known as the Personal Information Protection Law (PIPL), which came into effect on November 1, 2021. The PIPL provides better government control over the organisational data of Chinese individuals. The stark difference between all the above standards and this standard is the applicability zone. This is applicable globally for all Chinese citizens and does not confirm only the state boundaries.

11.5. PCI DSS

Payment Card Industry Data Security Standard (PCI DSS) is a global standard launched in 2004 by the five major financial organisations that are core to the credit card business namely Visa, Mastercard, American Express, Discover, and JCB. The PCI DSS standard was a strong response to a growing number of data breaches involving credit card data.

- The PCI DSS is a set of security standards that organisations must comply with in order to protect credit card data.
- The PCI DSS has 12 requirements that cover a wide range of security measures, such as physical security, network security, application security, and data security.
- The PCI DSS is enforced by payment card brands, acquiring banks, and governments globally. Organisations that are not compliant with the PCI DSS are not allowed to carry out payment businesses and also incur heavy penalties.
- The PCI DSS has been evolving since its inception in 2004. The latest version of the PCI DSS, version 3.2, was released in 2018 and a new release v4 is being published.

The PCI DSS is a constantly evolving standard. The PCI SSC (Security Standards Council) regularly publishes new guidance and resources to help organisations stay up-to-date on the latest security threats and best practices.

Here are some of the key milestones in the history of PCI:

- 2004: The PCI DSS is first released.
- 2006: The PCI SSC is formed.
- 2009: The PCI DSS is updated to version 1.2.
- 2013: The PCI DSS is updated to version 2.0.
- 2018: The PCI DSS is updated to version 3.2.
- 2023: The PCI DSS is expected to be updated to version 4.0.

11.6. The 12 Requirements of PCI DSS

1. Install and maintain a firewall configuration to protect cardholder data. This includes using a firewall to block unauthorised access to your network and to segment your network so that cardholder data is isolated from other types of data.
2. Do not use vendor-supplied default passwords. This includes passwords for your firewall, web server, database server, and any other system that stores or processes cardholder data.
3. Implement strong access controls to protect cardholder data. This includes using strong passwords, multi-factor authentication, and least privilege access.
4. Restrict access to cardholder data by `business need-to-know'. This means that only employees who need access to cardholder data in order to do their job should have access to it.
5. Identify and authenticate all system users. This includes using strong passwords, multi-factor authentication, and least privilege access.
6. Encrypt all cardholder data in transit and at rest. This includes encrypting cardholder data when it is being transmitted over a network and when it is stored on a system.
7. Regularly monitor and test networks and systems. This includes using intrusion detection systems, vulnerability scanners, and other tools to monitor your network and systems for security threats.

8. Maintain a policy that addresses information security for all personnel. This policy should include training requirements for all employees on security best practices and procedures.
9. Develop and maintain secure systems and applications. This includes using secure coding practices, implementing input validation, and patching software vulnerabilities.
10. Remain current with PCI DSS changes. The PCI DSS is regularly updated to reflect the latest security threats and best practices. It is important to stay up-to-date on the latest changes to the PCI DSS so that you can keep your organisation compliant.
11. Implement a process to regularly test and assess your security controls. This includes using penetration testing, vulnerability scanning, and other tools to test your security controls for effectiveness.
12. Maintain a documented information security policy and procedure. This documentation should include your organisation's security policies and procedures, as well as any supporting documentation, such as security plans, risk assessments, and incident response plans.

11.7 Benefits of PCI

Organisations that are not adhering to PCI DSS Compliance are subject to fines and other penalties from the payment card brands and acquirers. They are severely at risk of data breaches, which can damage their reputation and financial bottom line and more importantly compromise consumer financial details. Therefore it is essential to comply with PCI DSS.

The following four are the major benefits of PCI Certification:

1. Reduces the risk of data breaches: By following the PCI DSS, organisations can reduce the risk of their cardholder data being compromised in a data breach.
2. Protects customer data: The PCI DSS helps to protect customer data from unauthorised access, use, or disclosure.
3. Improves brand reputation: Being PCI compliant can help to improve an organisation's brand reputation by demonstrating that they are committed to protecting customer data.
4. Avoids fines and penalties: Organisations that are not compliant with the PCI DSS may be subject to fines and other penalties from the payment card brands.

11.8 Other Important Fintech Regulatory Standards

1. **ISO 27001:** This is an international standard that specifies the requirements for an information security management system (ISMS). An ISMS is a set of policies and procedures that organisations put in place to protect their information assets.
2. **PSD2:** The Payment Services Directive 2 (PSD2) is a regulation in EU law on payment services and payment service providers (PSPs). It was adopted in 2015 and came into effect in January 2018. The new version of the Payment Services Directive 2 (equivalent to PSD3) Payment Services Regulation (PSR) was adopted in June 2022. It is expected to come into effect in January 2025.

Summary

At times I feel that Fintech is a wild beast that can destroy because of the power and impact on the citizens of the world. This beast needs to be tamed so that the power of this beast can be harnessed for the betterment of humanity. This chapter covers this angle of taming the beast in a very brief. In this chapter we have covered the top standards built by global financial institutions by coming together. The primary motive of setting the standards is the data protection and security. These standards like PCI cover how data can be protected and secured while in transit as well as at rest. This regulatory sector is known as RegTech in the technology ecosystem. Based on my study of these regulatory standards prescribe standard operating procedures and also recommends the good practises that must be followed. The compliance of these regulatory standards is mandatory for very critical systems at the same time more tools and frameworks are required to be built for continuous assessment and compliance. Also we have seen regional standards like GDPR are covering the protection of the consumer considering the choice of the consumer to select what personal data can be shared, with whom and what purpose. All the regions and countries are adopting these types of standards. The latest entrant to this is India's "The Digital Personal Data Protection Bill, 2022". For further study I recommend to read this standard, this is available freely on government websites.

Financial data is like a navigation map; to reach your destination, you must not only understand the map but also know how to drive.

Chapter 12

Data Driven

Now at this point in time we are fully aware of the connected Fintech ecosystem. We have gone through multiple concepts and details of all the aspects of Fintech. We have all the relevant Fintech information stored in our brains. We are nearing the end of the book, and it is the perfect opportunity to discuss the data- a critical element in Fintech systems.

Fintech has always been a data-focused industry. This data analysis goes back to the 18th century when two Scottish ministers wanted to set up a life insurance fund in 1774. They partnered with a mathematician from the University of Edinburgh, collected statistical data, and applied mathematical models to their newly launched UK pension and life insurance company - Scottish Widows.

The area of Fintech data is characterised by its large volumes captured from different data sources. At the same time, there are technological developments in Cloud computing and Big Data analysis. We need to look into how this data can be stored, organised and made sense of.

Let us look at the different data storage models followed by their analysis.

12.1. Data Storage Models Applied to Fintech (Lake-Warehouse-Mart)

Data is the King in today's information age. Utilising data for reporting and reviewing relevant data in real-time, has never been the most important feature offered by Fintech organisations.

Data-driven decisions, aided by analytics, are crucial in an ever-competitive Fintech space. The clients are ready to opt for another provider if they don't get the right information from a Fintech organisation to make business decisions.

Traditionally, financial institutions and service companies have dealt with data in their respective divisions in a siloed manner, resulting in disjointed outcomes of business performance. This approach is not at all acceptable in today's data-driven world.

Fintech Data Analytics helps to enhance portfolios and make strategic decisions.

Business Intelligence (BI) solutions enable real-time decision-making with interactive, responsive and actionable visualisation. This has become a Fintech data ecosystem.

Fintech data engineering in itself is becoming a dedicated branch of the Fintech ecosystem. Fintech organisations are using Data engineering solutions to manage & govern complex data ecosystems and enhance data adoption. There are three major data storage models used to run data analytics.

12.2. Data Lakes

A data lake is a large, centralised repository of data that is collected from a variety of sources. It is a raw data repository that is not organised or structured in any way. This means that data lakes can contain a wide variety of data, including structured data, unstructured data, and semi-structured data.

Data lakes are used in Fintech for a variety of purposes, including:

1. **Data storage:** Data lakes can be used to store large amounts of data that would not be practical to store in a traditional database. This data can be used for a variety of purposes, such as data analysis, machine learning, and artificial intelligence once a pre-processing or pipeline is built on the data lake.
2. **Data correlation and exploration:** Data lakes can be used to explore data and identify patterns and trends across structured and unstructured data. This data correlation is used to improve business decision models.
3. **Data integration:** Data lakes can be used to integrate data from different sources. This data integration can be employed to create a unified view of the data to be used for a variety of purposes, such as fraud detection and risk assessment.
4. **Data governance:** Data lakes can be used to implement data governance policies. This data governance helps to ensure that data is secure, compliant, and accessible.

5. **Reduced data silos:** Data lakes can help to break down data silos. This means that data from different sources can be stored in a single repository, to be accessed by different departments and teams within a Fintech company. This can help to improve collaboration and communication within a Fintech company.
6. **Reduced data costs:** Data lakes can help to reduce data costs. This is because data lakes can store data in a more efficient way than traditional databases. This can save Fintech companies money on storage costs and data processing costs.

Data lakes are a valuable tool for Fintech companies. They help companies to store, explore, integrate, and govern data in a way that would not be possible with traditional databases. This can help companies to improve business decision-making, develop new products and services, and comply with regulations.

Data lakes store large amounts of data that would not be practical to store in a traditional database. This can help Fintech companies to collect and store more data, to be used for a variety of purposes - to build patterns and pipelines for data analysis, machine learning, and artificial intelligence.

12.3 Data Warehouses

A data warehouse is a structured centralised repository of data that is used for reporting and analysis. It is a collection of data that is integrated and organised for analysis.

Data warehouses are used in Fintech for a variety of purposes, including:

1. **Reporting:** Data warehouses are used to generate reports that provide insights into business performance. These reports can be used to track sales, identify trends, and make strategic decisions.
2. **Analysis:** Data warehouses are used to analyse data to identify patterns and trends. This analysis can be used to improve business processes, identify potential risks, and make better decisions.
3. **Data mining:** Data warehouses are used for data mining, which is the process of extracting hidden patterns and trends from data. This data mining can be used to identify new customers, target marketing campaigns, and improve customer service.
4. **Business intelligence:** Data warehouses are used for business intelligence (BI), which is the process of using data to improve decision-making. BI can be used to identify opportunities, solve problems, and make better decisions.
5. **Increased efficiency:** Data warehouses can help businesses save time and money by structurally centralising data and providing access to it from a single location. This reduces the need to duplicate data and the time it takes to access data from multiple sources.
6. **Increased compliance:** Data warehouses can help businesses comply with regulations by providing a central repository

of data that can be easily audited. This data can be used to demonstrate compliance with regulations such as the General Data Protection Regulation (GDPR) as we have seen in the regulatory section.

The key differences between a data warehouse and a data lake are in-

- **Data storage:** Data warehouses are typically used to store structured data, while data lakes can store a variety of data types, including structured, unstructured, and semi-structured data.
- **Data organisation:** Data warehouses are typically organised in a way that makes it easy to examine and analyse the data, while data lakes are typically stored in a raw format that is not organised in any way.
- **Data usage:** Data warehouses are typically used for reporting and analysis, while data lakes can be used for a variety of purposes, such as data exploration, machine learning, and artificial intelligence.
- **Data governance:** Data warehouses typically have more stringent data governance requirements than data lakes.

Data warehouses are better suited for businesses that need to store and analyse structured data for reporting and analysis purposes which is the cornerstone of the Fintech Data ecosystem.

12.4. Data Marts

A Data mart is a subset of a data warehouse that is designed to support a very specific business function. It is a nimble, focused repository of data that is tailored to the needs of a particular group of people or applications.

Here are some Key examples of data marts usage in Fintech

1. A bank may have a data mart that stores data about its customers' banking or credit card transactions. This data mart can be used to generate reports on customer spending habits, identify potential fraud, and target marketing campaigns.
2. A financial advisor may have a data mart that stores data about his client's investment portfolios. The purpose of this data mart can be to generate reports on client performance, identify potential risks, and make recommendations for investment changes.
3. Financial Application usage and efficiency the explosion of apps, as seen in earlier sections generates very specific customer usage and behaviour with Apps, which helps to optimise the functionality of the app offered.

Thus data marts can be used in a variety of ways to improve the efficiency, effectiveness, and profitability of Fintech businesses.

12.5 Active Data Decisions (ADDs)

Active data decision (ADD) refers to the process of using data to make decisions in real-time. This is in contrast to traditional decision-making, which typically involves gathering data, analysing it, and then making a decision.

Fintech ADDs are used in a variety of settings as follows:

1. **Customer service:** ADD can be used to provide personalised customer service by providing customer service representatives with real-time information about customers' needs and preferences.
2. **Fraud detection:** ADD can be used to detect fraud by analysing real-time data for patterns that may indicate fraudulent activity as discussed in subsequent sections.
3. **Risk assessment:** ADD can be used to assess risks by analysing real-time data for potential risks.
4. **Pricing:** ADD can be used to set prices in real-time by analysing real-time data about supply and demand.
5. **Inventory management:** ADD can be used to manage inventory by analysing real-time data about demand and supply.
6. ADD can help businesses to improve their efficiency, effectiveness, and profitability by making better decisions in real-time.
7. **Increased profitability:** ADD can help businesses to increase their profitability by making better decisions, improving efficiency, and reducing risk.

12.6 AI/ML Fintech ADD (Active Data Decision)

There are a variety of algorithms and AI/ML techniques that can be used for ADD. Some of the most common include:

1. **Machine learning:** Machine learning algorithms can be used to learn patterns in data and make predictions based on those patterns. This can be applied for a variety of ADD applications, such as fraud detection, risk assessment, and pricing.
2. **Natural language processing:** Natural language processing (NLP) algorithms can be used to understand human language. This can be used for a variety of ADD applications, such as customer service, marketing, and risk assessment.
3. **Computer vision:** Computer vision algorithms can be used to understand images and videos. This can be used for a variety of ADD applications, such as fraud detection, risk assessment, and marketing.
4. **Recommendation engines:** Recommendation engines can be used to recommend products or services to customers based on their past behaviour. This can be used for a variety of ADD applications, such as marketing and customer service.
5. **Chatbots:** Chatbots can be used to interact with customers in a natural language conversation. This can be applied to a variety of ADD applications, such as customer service and marketing.

The specific algorithm or AI/ML technique that is used will depend on the specific ADD application that would be addressed in the subsequent session.

12.7. Fraud Detection

Financial fraud is the unavoidable reality of the Fintech industry. As financial services are becoming easily accessible because of the advent of new technology. The goal for everyone is to minimise losses due to fraud.

- **Why do frauds happen?**

  Recently I came across a TV Show about espionage (India Disney Hotstar- Special Ops 1.5). A spy agent goes rogue and his motives are explained by the protagonist of the show. I saw an analogy between those motivations and financial fraud.

  In the same words, the motives of financial fraud would fall into one or many of these categories M.I.C.E. Which means: Money, Ideology, Coercion and Ego.

  This is very easy to understand for everyone.

  Which organisations can be more susceptible to these Financial Frauds?

  - Organisation offering financial services that are relatively successful and have a substantial number of consumers on the platform. That means financial fraud would happen on your platform if you as a company are valuable.
  - When services offered by organisations are picking up at a brisk pace resulting in wider media coverage
  - Organisations that have been an established brand for a substantial number of years and have started offering new financial services like an online portal, and online

payments which are attracting a new set of consumers on your platform And these new platforms are integrated with the existing established formats.

- Organisations based in a region or geographical area where the latest security standards are not adopted as mandatory requirements.

  Apart from these the major and the most important reason is when the end consumer is not educated to suspect malicious activities, be it phone calls, an inconspicuous-looking message or a lottery email.

  This is one of the most prevalent methods of instigating fraud. The service usage must be very easy at the same time very secure (easier said than done).

- **What are the ongoing trends to detect these Frauds?**

  Following are some of the basic techniques used to detect frauds.

  - **Behavioural Pattern for EWS (Early Warning System)**- This includes checking past activities and building a pattern
  - **Device Identification** - For online frauds generally this is the basic check to see if the same device is used to consume a service multiple times.
  - **Fake account identification** - Identifying if the email addresses, physical addresses are fake using external services. Especially using secured social engineering platforms.

- **Velocity Check** - how often the services are used, for how much monetary value.
- **One of the latest and effective techniques is "shadow banning"** - which effectively identifies fake access and lets the intruder access the system in a mock mode without actually impacting financially. This helps in obfuscating the fraud detection algorithm from the intruder.

Additionally, based on the data models, AI/ML algorithms can be used for fraud detection and risk management.

Following are typical fraud detection algorithms:

- **Decision trees:** Decision trees are a type of supervised learning algorithm that can be used to classify or predict data. They work by creating a tree-like structure of decisions, where each decision leads to a different outcome. Decision trees are often used for fraud detection and risk assessment in Fintech domains.
- **Support vector machines (SVMs):** SVMs are another type of supervised learning algorithm that can be used to classify or predict data. They work by finding the hyperplane (separation of two or more classes of data) that best separates two classes of data. SVMs are often used for fraud detection and risk assessment.
- **Random forests:** Random forests are an ensemble learning algorithm that combines multiple decision trees to make predictions. They are often used for fraud detection and risk assessment.

- **K-nearest neighbours (KNN):** KNN is a non-parametric, lazy learning algorithm that can be used for classification or regression. It works by finding the k most similar data points to a new data point and using those data points to make a prediction. KNN is often used for fraud detection and risk assessment.

12.8. Fintech Marketing Trends and Projections 2023-2024

The current market for Fintech apps is growing exponentially!

Did you know that ninety per cent of people use some form of Fintech app to handle their finances?

In fact, Americans utilise Fintech applications more than social media and video streaming applications.

Hard to believe in this age of social media dominance but true.

The increase in the number of people implies more market opportunities.

However, it also indicates increasing competition to obtain market share.

For example, there were 6,220 Fintech startups in the United Kingdom, 13,125 in India, and 71,153 in the United States.

The need to adapt and the convenience of contactless payments due to the COVID-19 pandemic drove the growth of Fintech and banking apps, but many new categories of Fintech apps have transformed in recent times.

Here are the top Fintech marketing trends you should watch out for this 2023.

Increased use of personalised communications

Numerous traditional banks and their policies don't reflect the needs of Gen Z and Millennials. They may want to provide better services or products, but rigid regulatory requirements and policies hinder them from doing so.

However, Fintech has leverage here. They can utilise data and technology to better understand their customers and personalise their offerings.

For instance, PerkFinance is creating a financial solution for the blue-collar workforce.

These days, Fintech firms can utilise data from different sources such as social media, CRM, and more to understand their user's financial situation and utilise that information to plan their Fintech marketing strategy.

Greater focus on digital marketing channels, such as social media

Over 4.5 billion individuals actively use social media. That means nine in ten online users use social media.

You can utilise social media to reach out to a wider audience. Nonetheless, if you have tried social media marketing before, you'll know it is not that simple.

Despite a generous number of followers, your posts hardly receive any engagement. Why? It may be because the content isn't compelling enough. Thus, you should take a strategic technique to drive engagement on your social media channels.

Determine the content type your audience wishes to consume on what platform. For instance, people wish to see and engage with videos and pictures on Instagram. Likewise, for conversations, online users prefer using Telegram or WhatsApp. After deciding, create and share content on those platforms.

Greater use of incentives to reward customers

Incentives are one of the major motivators in sales. Likewise, incentives could also ramp up your finance customer acquisition strategy.

Take the example of PayPal for instance, PayPal struggled to get customers in its initial days. It is not like they didn't market or try collaborations with banks. They did. However, nothing worked as anticipated.

Thus, they decided to incentivize their customers to drive organic and viral growth.

They gave $10 to new customers for signing up and gave $10 to existing customers for referrals. They spent $20 per new customer. With that strategy, they noticed seven to ten per cent daily organic growth.

Some ways in which you can incentivize your customers include offering cash rewards on accomplishing a milestone, giving joining bonuses, giving referral bonuses, and offering cash back.

More emphasis on bespoke financial services

As the pace of digital transformation continues to accelerate; new banking requirements will become more crucial to study throughout the next transition wave.

Thus, there will be more emphasis on the volume of bespoke financial services for customers. The fundamentals of digitising banking have been set, and thus, the industry can now concentrate on making and distributing new goods and services across devices and in real time.

As with other Fintech marketing trends, the concept of incorporating banking into social media apps and even the IoT is indicative of a change towards a more inclusive omnichannel strategy.

For bigger banks to be a part of their customers' lives, they should create banking into more than simply smartphones.

More focus on educating consumers

Financial literacy is vital. But only nineteen per cent of millennials see themselves as financially literate, although fifty-one per cent of them tend to utilise mobile payment apps.

Your Fintech marketing strategy must focus on educating consumers about different financial aspects. You can make bite-sized videos to educate them. Share on all possible channels, such as TikTok, Reels, YouTube, or your mobile app.

It will also help if you make evergreen content to establish brand authority. For instance, your blog page can be the go-to resource for anyone looking for specific financial advice.

Fintech growth is not slowing down. It can play a crucial role in filling the gap left by the traditional banking system while also improving its customer base.

Summary

- From the democratisation of finance, where technology has been literally brought to our doorstep, to decentralisation, there's been immense progress. The main component of Decentralised Finance (DeFi) is the blockchain, which ensures distributed control, low risk, and trust.
- One of the initiatives towards democratisation is ONDC (Open Network for Digital Commerce). It is a network of large and small scale, online and offline traders for a more centralised marketplace.
- A step ahead is metaverse, which is the freshest entry to Fintech. Synonymous with virtual banking, metaverse uses virtual tools and technology in the finance and banking industry.
- As there are two sides of a coin, everything has its pros and cons, so also a drawback of Fintech is that it is susceptible to fraudulent practices.
- The solution for this is fraud detection methods, like, behavioural patterns, device identification, fake account identification and velocity check.

Simplifying financial interactions enhances human relations.

Chapter 13

Fintech Design Thinking: The Way Forward

The Fintech industry is one of the prolifically growing industries in the world today. This is the reason it is attracting a lot of talent along with companies and investors.

However, as I have seen it up close, I can safely say that the growth is haphazard, which was in a way, actually the need.

The traditional Fintech models were inept, slow and inefficient from the perspective of the modern users of financial services.

In this book, I have attempted to track part of the digital payments evolution over half a century, as this is the cornerstone of all industries.

This is, anyways not a concise history book =, but instead, a milestone map which has driven the Fintech industry.

The book helps address the following basic questions.

- What was the need for the payment instruments over and above cash?
- What problems did the industry face?

- What were the suitable solutions?

The book also explains the digital payment arising trends and technologies that are guiding the current Fintech models.

These are driven by technology giants as well as startup ecosystems alike.

The Fintech ecosystem provides opportunities for all enthusiasts to get involved and contribute towards the evolutionary cycle of the industry.

While journeying through this book, let's together seek to find answers to the following:

- What were the path-breaking ways in which digital payments have driven the Fintech industry forward?
- How are the technology giants involved in the Fintech industry?
- What are the new tech trends that are and will be crucial in charting the future of Fintech?

One of the main problems I encountered while researching and working on the book is the lack of consolidated models where one can recognize different domains under the Fintech umbrella.

To bridge that gap, the book specifically lists some of the key domains of Fintech.

This will give clarity to the reader about the current prevailing models for different domains.

The domains in consideration are the ones that are creating the most impact such as- Shared Economy, Insuretech, Wealthtech, E-commerce, Lendtech etc..

Are these the only domains?

A logical question indeed.

Certainly not! And that is the simple answer.

There are umpteen number of business models under Fintech, though these are the prominent ones used in everyday life and like I said, these are the ones making the most ripples and waves and generating the most impact.

The book illustrates the different entities involved in these models and their interaction to make the models work especially around the area of the following questions.

1. How does the share economy work?
2. What are the typical Insurtech and Wealthtech models in use?
3. How are the Ecom solutions modelled?
4. We have already studied and understood the 5D model of
    - **i.** Democratise
    - **ii.** Decentralisation
    - **iii.** Disruption
    - **iv.** Directive Regulatory
    - **v.** Data Driven

We talked about the evolution, arising trends, technologies along with the organisations within the Fintech ecosystem. Also, we have discussed in detail the models being developed and used to address problems in the Fintech domain.

And then we looked at the Fintech Future models.

As we go through the current evolving models we the realise following:

1. There are a lot of common features across models, e.g. KYC, Fraud check etc.
2. Each of the Fintech domains must have these common features
3. These features can be sub-categorised into multiple business value features, business support features, technology features etc.
4. New industry use case needs must have these features to be used, be it a Big Tech or a startup

We learned that the current prevailing problems with these models are

1. No common interface
2. No common cloud platform framework
3. None or very minimal sharing components across the industry
4. Features are global, but standards are regional
5. Every company implements it in a very bespoke fashion in a very siloed mode

6. Although there are standards like ISO20022, the standardisation is limited to specific business transactions and not covering the overall end-to-end business use cases
7. The standards and compliances are fragmented
8. The development of new business scenarios takes a lot of time, making the whole Fintech industry progress laggard.

Reviewing & Overviewing all this brings us to one logical conclusion-

That to be successful on all parameters Fintech needs to create a paradigm shift by adopting a design thinking approach as the way forward.

13.1. Design Thinking

I want to share something very important and very relevant with you. I have been reading a very good book by Dr. Srinidhi K. Parthasarathi. The book's name is gita@workspace.

This book relates real-life situations, especially in professional life to the verses of the Gita showing us how the Bhagavad Gita is still most relevant to our daily life.

There is a topic discussed in this book on transformation, and I felt it really can be applied to Fintech transformation.

सर्वस्य चाहं हृदि सन्निविष्टो

मत्तः स्मृतिर्ज्ञानमपोहनञ्च।

वेदैश्च सर्वैरहमेव वेद्यो

वेदान्तकृद्वेदविदेव चाहम्।। १५-१५।।

Meaning

The assimilation of the knowledge cycle goes through three phases. In the first unknown or unforgetful state - the state of 'apohanam', the absence of memory. Next, we learn & know something, knowledge happens, and this is 'jnyaanam'.

Knowledge is preserved in the memory, the `smrithi'.

All these steps, towards the acquisition of knowledge happen due to Ishvara, who is seated in our intellect, poetically referred to as `hridi' or intellect. Then the cycle continues, so for learning anything new, we need to forget the existing knowledge and construct/reconstruct the understanding in a different form as the process of knowledge acquisition.

[*Apohanam* (Divergence thorough forgetfulness) > *Dnyanam* (Convergence)]

A typical example is Milk transforming to Curd over time. After this transformation, the curd is churned adding water. This process can be considered a destructive or a divergence of curd into outward flux, creating buttermilk.

Either the buttermilk can be consumed, or the next cycle of churning continues. The next outcome is the butter which essentially is a reconstruction of milk by the process of destruction and reconstruction.

This in essence is the Design Thinking Approach. Reconstruction by destruction or deconstruction of existing constructs consciously.

The Picture below represents this design thinking process at a high level.

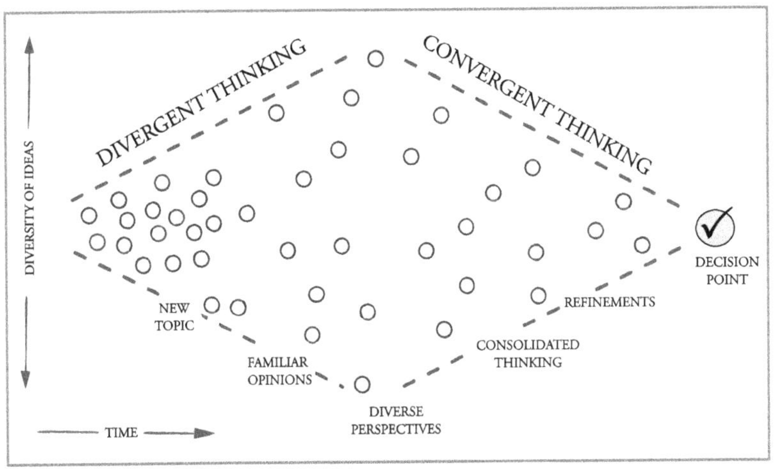

Source: blogs.elon.edu

Applying Design Thinking to Fintech

We have seen multiple considerations and impediments related to the existing Fintech models. Also, we reviewed the 5D model which is a prevailing model that is evolving and being applied to the existing Fintech systems.

How can we put these 5D aspects of Fintech through a churn and contemplate a process of Divergence using the Design Thinking approach?

The goal of this process is

1. Challenging and questioning the status quo of Fintech mechanisms as they stand

2. Eliminating noise from the existing Fintech processes
3. Unlearning the dated Fintech process
4. Identifying the areas of insufficiency and archaic methods
5. Analysing and synthesising the 5D Fintech model
6. Ultimately creating a better set of choices
7. Reviewing the choices with local acumen
8. Exploring tools and techniques
9. Focusing on the choice
10. Flinalising & fleshing out the details

It is my sincere intention that this book ignites in you the desire to diverge to converge and impact many lives through your work in the Fintech domain irrespective of what capacity you are connected to it in.

On this note let us together start working towards the convergence process.

Together it is our responsibility to re-think and re-build the Fintech ecosystem to have far-reaching positive consequences.

And this book is merely a ripple in the vast ocean of Fintech. Together we can create a wave of impact. Thank you for staying with me. Now, let's get to work.

NOTES:

NOTES:

www.ingramcontent.com/pod-product-compliance
Ingram Content Group UK Ltd.
Pitfield, Milton Keynes, MK11 3LW, UK
UKHW021706190726
13853UKWH00001B/435

9 789355 547064